HOW TO WORK WITH DOGS

In this Series

Other titles in preparation

WORK WITH DOGS

A practical careers guide for everyone

Pauline Appleby

How To Books

Author's Dedication

For David, James and Richard

British Library Cataloguing in Publication Data
A catalogue record for this book is available from the British Library.

© Copyright 1995 by Pauline Appleby.

First published in 1995 by How To Books Ltd, Plymbridge House, Estover Road, Plymouth PL6 7PZ, United Kingdom. Tel: Plymouth (01752) 735251/ 695745. Fax: (01752) 695699. Telex: 45635.

Note: The material contained in this book is set out in good faith for general guidance and no liability can be accepted for loss or expense incurred as a result of relying in particular circumstances on statements made in the book. The law and regulations are complex and liable to change, and readers should check the current position with the relevant authorities before making personal arrangements.

Typeset by Concept Communications (Design & Print) Ltd, Crayford, Kent.
Printed and bound by The Cromwell Press Ltd, Broughton Gifford, Melksham, Wiltshire.

Contents

LIST OF ILLUSTRATIONS

Preface

'What do you want to do when you leave school, Pauline?'
'I want to work with dogs'.
'But that's not a career; what do you want to do as a career?'

This was the kind of encouragement I received when I was preparing to leave school. Sadly, it can sometimes be the case today, although I'm sure that these days (up until now) it has been a case of the information not being readily available rather than lack of interest. Fortunately for me I had very supportive and understanding parents who allowed me to follow my own choice. What I didn't know then was what a vast range of choices there were.

The purpose of this book is to show the reader the many choices available, which ones are realistic options for you to pursue, which offer plenty of opportunity and conversely which have a limited scope, whether qualifications are required, and which key personal qualities are sought.

All of the details about the organisations mentioned are correct at the time of going to press and have been approved by those organisations. The case studies that follow many of the options provide a personal view of those roles. They are based on real life and are about the people who carry out those roles. Useful addresses appear after relevant sections and you will find more at the end of the book.

Many of the organisations that have been covered vary in different areas of the country (for example Dog Wardens) so where this is relevant I have concentrated on one particular location. The details of staff allocation, working practices etc may vary elsewhere but it still provides a good insight into the type of set-up you might expect.

One thing that was very apparent to me whilst researching this book was the pride, dedication and job satisfaction that shone out from the people I interviewed. I felt very fortunate in being able to meet so many colourful characters and was fascinated by the history of some of the organisations covered. I am very grateful to all those who gave me their time and who shared their knowledge and experience with me, in particular all of the case studies that appear throughout the book. I would also like to acknowledge the help of the following people in the preparation of this book:

Rebecca Addison (WCPN), Jeff Martin (HM Customs & Excise), Annette Chinn (NCDL), Suzy Graham (RSPCA), Steve Allen (HM Prisons), Inspector Stuart Holder (West Midlands Police), Mick Foster & Les Price (British Transport Police), Lieutenant-Colonel Duncan Green (Battersea), Linda Hams (DFD), Clive Gilmore & Flight Sergeant Bob Warren (RAF), Captain John Corbin (RAVC), Andrea Frazer (Blue Cross), Sarah Heath MRCVS, Dr Anthony Podberscek, Michael Quinney (Wood Green) and Dr Anne McBride.

I am also indebted to Bev Preston for her input, to those who kept me going, Caroline, Clive, Cathy and Shelagh; to my husband, David, for his editorial assistance, to my assistant, Jayne, for 'holding the fort' whilst I was writing this, and to Roger Ferneyhough for having faith in the project from the start.

Pauline Appleby

1
Starting a Career with Dogs

WOULD YOU ENJOY WORKING WITH DOGS?

Some people enjoy dogs as a hobby and turn their interest into a career. Many school leavers desperately want to work with animals and choose working with dogs as their first option. Some adults decide on a career change later in life and find the idea of working with dogs appealing. Some work with dogs as part of another job function, for example, Police Dog Handlers; they are Policemen first and later specialise to become Police Dog Handlers. Sometimes people already working with dogs professionally seek a change of career but want to be able to continue to work with dogs.

These days training schemes and recognised qualifications can lead to excellent and varied career prospects. Examples of the types of job available are: professional groomers, guide dog trainers, dog wardens, and journalists to name but a few. The pet trade industry employs thousands of people from all walks of life in all sorts of ways. All of these jobs have requirements that need to be met; in some cases qualifications are required. Of course, when making choices career prospects and job satisfaction are important factors to consider. This book will help you look at the wide range of career and job opportunities available.

This chapter covers aspects of where to look for jobs, how to prepare your application and guidance for interview techniques. Later chapters detail what each job involves, their day to day function and a short history of the organisation where applicable. In many cases there is a personal account in the form of 'A day in the life of. . .'

Wherever possible, the job descriptions highlight

- Experience required

- Qualities looked for by the employer

- Qualifications available

- Career prospects

- Contact addresses and telephone numbers where appropriate and

- Self-employment potential

so that you can find the information you need at a glance.

Would a career with dogs suit me?

Not everyone is suited to working with dogs. There are some personality traits that are very important and to be fair to yourself you should assess your qualities and decide whether working with dogs is really for you. The first thing that springs to mind is to have a natural empathy with dogs. This doesn't mean that you need years of dog ownership behind you, but you must feel comfortable in their company and have a general understanding of their ways.

Equally important is an empathy with people. In most jobs, the dogs that you will be involved with will, in one way or another, *belong* to someone; that someone is not going to let you be involved with their pet if they don't take to you themselves and so interpersonal skills should never be overlooked. Working with dogs is not, in many cases, a way of escaping from having to deal with people. For example, the first chance to impress a client in most businesses is on the telephone. If staff are either unable to communicate well or seem unfriendly or uncooperative then it is highly unlikely that the enquiry will result in a booking. Likewise, assistance dogs are first and foremost an aid to improving the quality of life for disabled people.

Of course, some people want to work with dogs because they prefer their company to that of people. If this is the case with you, then you may still be able to find a job that suits you, but you will be more restricted in your options. It may also be worth having a think about why you feel that way and consider a training course that will help you improve the problem areas.

Other skills which may seem unrelated at first also have their uses and will help persuade employers that you are the person for them; basic book keeping/accounting (obviously important if you intend to start your own business), organisational skills, ability to communicate well with others, initiative, are examples.

Working conditions

Working conditions vary enormously from job to job. Most, however, involve working outdoors in all weathers, hot, cold, wet and windy. Will you remain just as keen and committed whatever the weather? For some people noise can be a problem, particularly if working in a large kennel establishment. It may seem an obvious inconvenience, but could you stand dogs barking apparently non-stop every working day? As with all animals, what goes in must come out, and when it comes out it needs to be shovelled up and put somewhere — could you deal with the messy end of things? Do you mind handling and preparing the dogs' food, often fresh meat? Are you physically fit? Dogs, of course, need to be walked, and some jobs mean they have to be walked a long way for exercise and/or training.

Would you really like your hobby to become your way of life, or would you rather keep a hobby as a hobby?

Coping with allergies

Some people find that they are allergic to dog hair. However, this need not be a problem as in many job functions you would be working outdoors, which often alleviates the problem (seek your GP's advice). Of course there are some jobs which do not necessitate coming into physical contact with dogs at all.

Self-assessment quiz

The following is a self assessment chart that will help you look at yourself and take a detached view of your suitability for working with dogs.

Score A, B or C (A = Very, B = Fairly, C = Not at all).

Question	*Rate yourself*
Are you interested in dogs?	_____
Are you interested in people?	_____
Are you fit?	_____
Are you caring?	_____
Are you informed?	_____
Are you prepared to work in all weathers?	_____
Are you prepared to put up with a lot of noise?	_____

Are you prepared to get your hands dirty?   ——————

How well do you get on with other people?   ——————

Are you prepared to cut up and handle meat?   ——————

Do you use your initiative well?   ——————

Are you self motivated?   ——————

Do you have an affinity with animals?   ——————

Are you able to work as part of a team?   ——————

If needed, are you capable of walking long
distances every day?   ——————

Are you a patient person?   ——————

Are you reliable?   ——————

Comments
If you score mainly As, then you are likely to be well suited to a job
with dogs.

If you score some Bs and some As, then you could be suited to
some jobs, but decide carefully which ones.

If you score mainly Cs, then a career with dogs is unlikely to
leave you feeling fulfilled and happy.

QUALIFICATIONS AND EXPERIENCE

The job function descriptions in Part 2 will give you information about
each particular job's requirements. Remember, the broader your range
of skills the more choice you will ultimately have to do whichever job
you like. For example, when making subject choices at school or college, think further ahead than just working with dogs. Skills such as
typing, computer studies, accounting/book-keeping, interpersonal skills
will all greatly improve your chances of a managerial position, and will
be particularly important if you aim to become self-employed at some
stage of your career. Take advantage of all the experience you can
while you are still a student as it may well be free and you are likely to
have more time to do the studying without pressure.

Of course, if you decide later in life that you'd like to acquire these skills, there are many college courses available for the mature student. Figure 1 shows a typical list of useful courses available at one college — Can you think of any others?

Jobs such as journalism, secretarial work and so on may need training before specialising into your chosen area of dogs.

Do I need work experience?

There is nothing as good for your CV as hands-on practical experience. A positive boon to a potential employer is to find that the applicant has done the job, or something similar before, even if only briefly. There are hundreds of boarding and rescue kennels all over the country which may welcome an extra pair of hands, especially during the summer months.

Hands on experience will provide you with a number of good opportunities:

1. To see if you really do feel comfortable being around dogs all day.

2. To gain some knowledge of the breeds, temperaments, body language and to improve your handling skills.

3. To prove to your potential employer that you can handle the work/weather conditions.

4. To make contacts which could prove useful in your career.

5. To help identify which areas you are competent in, and which require further work.

How to get work experience

School or college
Work experience is often offered in the last year of school or college. These placements can be used for references and may be an opportunity for you to gain experience in an organisation that you would otherwise not be able to gain access to, so use the opportunity wisely.

Local opportunities
Figures 3 and 4 are examples of letters to local boarding kennels or rescue kennels asking for a placement. They are examples of requests for a paid and a voluntary position.

Useful courses typically available at local colleges

Book-keeping & Accounting Pt I
Book-keeping & Accounting Pt II
Sage Computerised Accounting
Introduction to Computers
Basic Computing Workshop
RSA Certificate in Counselling Skills
First Aid — Basic
First Aid — At Work
Health & Safety Short Courses
Top Quality Management
Office Skills/Administration
Intensive Secretarial Level 1
Modern Office Technology
Intermediate Photography
Signing for the Deaf
Teaching
Typing/Keyboarding
Psychology
Business Studies
Biology

Fig. 1. Useful college courses.

How to get qualifications

Some positions will require you to have certain qualifications before you will be considered. Some offer on-job training and in-house qualifications in related areas, and others require none at all.

Local colleges
A **BTec Certificate and Diploma in Animal Care** is available at some local colleges. The list on page 16 is accurate at the time of going to press but could change from year to year, so do check with your local college.

Evening courses
Local colleges run courses for people who are unable to attend during the day, *ie* mothers with young children, and full time employed people.

Private college
Bellmead Training School for kennel staff is part of Battersea Dogs

Home and trains students in all areas of kennel work, including management, grooming and breeding. See the entry under kennel assistants for further details (page 28). There may be other establishments around the country which advertise training courses from time to time. Advertisements would be found in the weekly dog publications, *Our Dogs* and *Dog World*.

University
Many universities offer degree courses in animal related subjects. The resulting qualifications can enhance your career prospects and earning potential enormously. These subjects include ethology, zoology and biology. Check your local library for guides to courses run by each university.

Open Learning Courses
The **Animal Care College** offers correspondence courses in the following:

1. General Certificate of Canine Studies — a foundation course in the administration, the showing, breeding, judging and understanding the world of show dogs.

2. Canine/Human Interface — an introduction to dog behaviour and training techniques for those involved in dog training, obedience, agility and trials.

3. Judging Diploma — an introduction into the art and science of judging dogs for breed specialists and all rounders.

4. The Dog Breeding Certificate — an introduction to the art, science and practice of dog breeding.

5. Veterinary Nursing Correspondence course.

6. Kennel Staff & Kennel Management training — the National Small Animal Care Certificate is designed for young people in their first year or so of kennel work and for those on employment training courses. The Diploma of Kennel Management is for those who feel that they would benefit from advanced study of management techniques applied to kennels.

7. National Small Animal Care Certificate.

BTEC FIRST CERTIFICATE/DIPLOMA IN ANIMAL CARE

One year full time
Lincolnshire College of Agriculture & Horticulture
Bishop Burton College of Agriculture
North East Surrey College of Technology
Camberley College of Agriculture & Horticulture
Carmarthenshire College of Technology & Art
Sparsholt College
Lancashire College of Agriculture & Horticulture
Pencoed College
Reaseheath College
Derbyshire College of Agriculture & Horticulture
Bicton College of Agriculture
Dorset College of Agriculture & Horticulture
Gloucester College of Agriculture
West Sussex College of Agriculture & Horticulture
Hartpury College — Gloucester
Brooksby College, Melton Mowbray

BTEC NATIONAL DIPLOMA IN ANIMAL CARE

Two years full time
Bicton College of Agriculture
Gloucester College of Agriculture
Sparsholt College
Bishop Burton College of Agriculture
Lancashire College of Agriculture & Horticulture
Pencoed College
Staffordshire College of Agriculture

ANIMAL CARE SVQ LEVEL 2

Elmwood College, Carslogie Road, Cupar, Scotland.
Tel: (01334) 52781.

This list is correct at time of going to press but please check details with your local college in case of changes.

Fig. 2. Colleges offering BTec Animal Care courses.
(Source: *Occupations '94*, Department of Employment)

Further details are available from: The Animal Care College, Ascot House, High Street, Ascot, Berks SL5 7JG.

HOW TO LOOK FOR A JOB

Where to look

Local papers
The Situations Vacant columns often appear once a week, but can be more often. Apply straightaway and follow the instructions for applications carefully. For example if it says write, don't phone.

Local shops
If you know there are kennels or an appropriate work place nearby.

Job centres
Check frequently — jobs go quickly here.

Youth Credits
Youth Credits are a vocationally based training route offering work experience and qualifications to at least NVQ2 standard. Your local Careers Service will be able to give you more details of how the scheme is run in your area.

Dog press
Our Dogs and *Dog World* are published every Friday and are available in most larger newsagents. They both have situations vacant columns and advertise jobs abroad as well as nationally. They may also have situations wanted columns, giving you the opportunity to briefly describe your experience, location (or willingness to move to a new area), age, type of situation you are looking for and so on, in the hope that you are just the person the reader is looking for!

Details of current courses and seminars will also be found in these journals.

Work experience placements
The employer will already know you and your capabilities/potential — ask them if they would consider you returning.

Friends and family
Many people you know will actually use a kennel/groomer for themselves.

On spec applications
Local kennels may not have vacancies immediately, but if your letter of application and CV stand out from the rest (and they get many) they may well contact you as and when a vacancy arises (the turn-over of kennel staff tends to be quite high). This has its advantages for the employer, who does not have to go to the expense of advertising and interviewing unsuitable applicants. Some organisations, such as The Dogs' Home Battersea and the Transport Police, keep their on spec applications on file and refer to them when having a recruitment drive. However, some other organisations do not welcome on spec applications, so it would be advisable to phone and check before writing.

How to write an application

When making an initial or on spec enquiry by letter, make sure that the reader's first impression of it is that it is written or typed neatly without spelling mistakes, that it is concise, that the reason for the letter is clear, and the information you have given is relevant.

In the vast majority of cases, advertisements will invite the reader to phone or write for an application form. If asked to complete an application form, remember that this is not a mere formality. What you put on the form may make the difference between being offered an interview and receiving a rejection letter. Even if you attach a copy of your CV, try to complete as much of the form as you can. It can be very irritating to an employee to read 'see enclosed CV' in every section.

Application forms can vary from simple one page documents to 22 pages of questions, such as the standard Police Force application form. Whichever type of form is used, the employer will have set the questions to find out specific information — so do not miss out any questions thinking they are irrelevant to you unless told to do so.

Keep a photocopy of your application form so you can refresh your memory of the information asked for and given when it comes to your interview.

Make sure that your answers are legible and that the application arrives in good, clean condition.

Preparing your curriculum vitae (CV)

The purpose of your curriculum vitae (CV) is to catch the eye of the employer, to arouse their curiosity about you and to make them want to interview you. It should be very neat, concise and immaculately

2 Glebe Hill
Woodrich
Worcestershire
WR5 6AJ

12th March 199X

Miss D Richards
Welford Rescue Society
Welford Road
Worcester
Worcs
WR8 0UB

Dear Miss Richards

I am interested in working with dogs as a career and I am currently seeking an opportunity to gain some work experience to enhance my career prospects.

I am writing to ask if you have any voluntary positions available for which I might be considered. I am happy to walk the dogs, clean their kennels, or anything else you might consider me suitable for. I am prepared to work in all weathers and I am available at weekends and during the school holidays. I would be happy to come and introduce myself to you whenever convenient.

My family has always owned dogs; we currently have two Cocker Spaniels, and I am very interested in learning more about them.

I look forward to hearing from you and enclose a stamped addressed envelope for your reply.

Yours sincerely

James Davis

Fig. 3. Letter applying for a voluntary position.

Amberley
Church Road
Leominster
Worcestershire
WR54 5AB

24th March 199X

Mrs J Miller
Top Hat Boarding Kennels
Cleeve Road
Leominster
Worcestershire
WR6 9UJ

Dear Mrs Miller

I am very keen to work with dogs as a career and I am currently seeking an opportunity to gain some experience during the two years I have left at school.

I am writing to ask if you have any part time positions available for which I might be considered. I would be available every weekend and during the school holidays and would be prepared to work in all weathers. I would be happy to walk the dogs, clean the kennels or do anything else you thought suitable.

I do have some experience with our family dogs, two Cocker Spaniels, but would like to broaden this experience. I am a bright, motivated girl and could supply you with personal references if required.

I enclose an SAE for your reply. I look forward to hearing from you.

Yours sincerely

Katherine Marston

Fig. 4. Letter applying for a part-time position.

presented. If you are not a competent typist yourself, it is well worth paying a professional typist or secretary to type it for you.

Keep it short and to the point
Your CV should not be a long and rambling document — one or two sides of A4 paper is plenty. It should include personal details — such as your name, address, telephone number and date of birth — as well as information about your education, qualifications and work experience. You may also wish to give details of your hobbies and interests and to name one or two people who have agreed to provide references. An example is shown in figure 5 but remember this is only a suggestion, and you should adapt the CV to your own requirements.

Your contact details
Let's look more closely at the information in your CV. Your name and address should be written in full — don't forget your postcode! — and *always* include a daytime telephone number, otherwise you may miss out on the chance of an interview. List any qualifications you have (and the grades if they are good ones) or name the subjects you studied and the courses you have undertaken.

Your work history
List your work experiences next, starting with your most recent job. Include your employer's name, dates of employment and your job title. Describe your main responsibilities briefly and don't fall into the trap of providing a long list of your many duties. The reader will have reached the boredom threshold before they reach the end of the page! Remember that your prospective employer may have read two hundred applications. Yours will need some real impact and sparkle if you are to stand out. Try using bullet points to summarise your achievements and successes. You can select and emphasise the skills and experiences which are particularly relevant to the job in question and gloss over those which are not so relevant.

Be specific. Instead of saying, 'I have wide experience of kennel work', say, 'I have eight years' experience providing sole care for up to fifteen dogs and ten cats in boarding kennels'.

You may feel that you have little experience, or that your experience isn't relevant. Consider including a section which summarises everything which is special about you — not only your experience but also your training or qualifications, your skills and aptitudes and

CURRICULUM VITAE

Name: Pat Rogers

Address: 2 Park Road
                               Sonning
                               Berkshire
                               RG12 9T

Telephone no. Daytime: (01734) 22748
              Evening: (01734) 40476

Date of birth: 25 January 1974

Nationality: British

Driving licence: Full, clean licence

Education: Fullbrook High School, Reading
                               1985 — 1990

                               4 CSE passes (History, Art,
                               Mathematics, French)
                               2 GCSE passes (English Language,
                               Biology)

Qualifications: I am currently studying for the
                               BTEC in Business & Finance at
                               evening classes

Work experience: October 1990 to date
                               Tweeville Boarding Kennels
                               Kennel Assistant

Skills: My work experience and college
                               training has helped me develop the
                               following:

                               *keyboarding skills (I have taken
                                an evening course in basic
                                computer literacy)

                               *organisational ability (set up a
                                computer-based client data-base;
                                plan rosters and holiday charts)

	*sound understanding of accounting principles and payroll preparation for the small firm
Hobbies:	I am a keen wildlife photographer and I enjoy showing my two Cocker Spaniels and helping to run my local club's annual exemption shows
References:	Mr G McCulloch Tweeville Boarding Kennels Haversham RG12 5RT Tel: (01734) 65478
	Miss N Warren Secretary — Haversham Kennel Society 11 Dorett Road Haversham RG15 8PY Tel: (01734) 66789
Reasons for applying for this post:	During my four years at Tweeville, I have gained all-round experience in the day-to-day management of a boarding kennels and I currently work with very little supervision. I also take bookings from clients, both in person and by telephone.
	I am keen to pursue a career in kennel management and hope to widen my experience by working within rescue kennels and by supervising other staff.
	I am a cheerful and enthusiastic worker. I have my own transport and I am willing to work in the evenings or at weekends as necessary.
	I feel my work experience, backed up by my accounts knowledge and organisational ability, would make me a useful team member, and I look forward to the opportunity of discussing this further at an interview.

Fig. 5. An example CV.

your personal qualities. Draw on the knowledge you gained at school or college, in clubs or societies, on committees, during Saturday jobs or voluntary work.

Using your hobbies and interests
Describing your hobbies and interests is another way to make your CV stand out. Don't just make a brief list. Reading, gardening and keeping fish won't make you memorable. Be specific and expand into sentences. 'I enjoy reading science fiction stories and growing patio plants, and I am particularly keen on breeding guppies and koi carp.' Even if there are twenty applicants who all have the same qualifications and experience as yourself, you will be the one who sticks in the employer's mind! If your hobby has helped you develop a useful skill (such as organising events, keeping a budget, or writing a newsletter) mention this too.

Giving references
You may wish to name one or two referees. Ask their permission before using their names and include their telephone numbers if possible. If you have work experience, you would be wise to include your present or most recent employer. Otherwise, you could name a teacher or college tutor or someone who can describe your abilities. For example, if you had experience organising the local church play-group, you could ask the vicar or priest, or if you have a Saturday job in a pet store, you could ask the shop manager. If you do not want your present employer contacted, state this very clearly within the references section. If you attach a separate note, it may become detached or be overlooked.

Making a final check
Finally, when you have finished your CV, check it, double-check it and get someone else to check it for errors, omissions and spelling mistakes. Start compiling your CV now. Don't wait until you see the job of your dreams advertised in the local paper. A good CV needs plenty of time and attention. Take a photocopy before you post it off with your covering letter so that you can refresh your memory when you are invited for an interview.

Note: *How to Apply for A Job* in this series gives more detailed help on preparing a CV.

Attending for interview
Finally, it's your chance to impress the employer and show that you

are the one they've been looking for. In a small business, your interview may be quite an informal affair — perhaps a quick tour of the premises and a one to one chat about your experience. In larger organisations, you may have a more formal interview by a panel of managers. Some organisations hold special selection weekends or assessment centres where you may be asked to undertake aptitude tests to see how well you match up to what they are looking for. Whatever the nature of your interview, if you don't understand a question or an instruction, ask for clarification.

The key to a successful interview is sound preparation.

- **Prepare to be punctual**. Try a dummy run to make quite sure you know the route and can find somewhere to park. A busy employer will not be impressed if you are late and arrive flustered and breathless.

- **Prepare your appearance**. Wear something smart but comfortable. Old jeans and wellies may be appropriate in some working environments when you've got the job, but you're not there yet! Care in your appearance will suggest care in your work.

- **Prepare your entrance**. The first four minutes of your interview are crucial in making a good impression. Whilst waiting for your appointment, take several deep breaths and picture yourself in the interview situation, answering confidently. When you meet the interview panel, smile, shake hands firmly, maintain steady eye contact and don't fiddle with your jewellery, your clothes, your hands or your hair. Keep your hands loosely folded in your lap. Try to remember that your interviewer may be just as nervous as you!

- **Anticipate the sort of questions** you may be asked and prepare your answers. Rehearse them out loud during the few days before your interview. The following are common interview questions:

What do you know about us?
What sort of experience do you have?
What do you think are the most important qualities for this job?
Why do you want this job?
What are your strengths and weaknesses?
What would you do if . . . there was a fire in the kennels? . . .
there was a dog fight? . . . one of the dogs went missing when

no-one else was there? . . . you took a telephone call from a client who was angry at the way her dog had been looked after?

- **Your reasons.** Be quite clear in your mind why you want to work with dogs. 'Because I don't like people' or 'I dunno really . . . I just like them' will not help your case. Avoid answering 'yes' or 'no'. Be ready to expand your replies and offer examples of what you have done or what you would do in a given situation. It is not helpful to criticise your present or previous employers, however much you may be tempted!

- Take along any **relevant documents** such as your qualifications, certificates or your NVQ Record of Achievement.

- Do your **homework on the organisation** and prepare a few relevant questions to show your interest.

If the position has been advertised as live-in, make sure that you are offered the opportunity to inspect the living quarters. These could vary tremendously from a mobile home to a private flat. Will you be sharing the accommodation with others? What are you expected to pay for in terms of rent, electricity, telephone etc?

Leave your interview on a positive note. Smile again and thank the interviewer for seeing you. Ask when you may expect to hear from them. If you are unsuccessful, ask if they can offer you any feedback or advice to help you in your next application.

2
'Hands On' Jobs

In this chapter we will discuss some of the 'hands on' jobs available to people wishing to work with dogs. In particular we will look at:

- kennel assistant
- professional groomer
- dog wardens
- veterinary nurses
- veterinary surgeons
- professional dog trainers
- pet behaviour counsellors
- search and rescue dog handlers

KENNEL ASSISTANTS

The job
The title of Kennel Assistant covers a multitude of job functions depending on where the position is held.

There are some basic elements of the job that will be common to all, and are as follows:

1 To care for the dogs in kennels.
2 To exercise the dogs.
3 Preparation and distribution of feeds.
4 Cleaning kennels and runs.
5 Grooming and bathing dogs.
6 Looking out for signs of ill health.
7 Caring for sick dogs.
8 Telephone/reception duties.

In most kennel establishments, weekend working will be necessary, as will working during bank holidays. In boarding kennels the busiest times are during traditional holiday periods, which means it will be unlikely that you would be able to take holidays at that time.

There are some positive points! Some experience with dogs would prove beneficial to a vast majority of other dog-related jobs and the vast number of boarding, rescue and quarantine kennels ensures that there are usually plenty of opportunities to gain that invaluable experience. You would be guaranteed the opportunity to handle all kinds of breeds and temperaments which would enable you to develop your handling skills and breed recognition skills.

You would be working mostly outdoors in all weathers (although it should not be forgotten that this includes beautiful spring days as well as dull winter ones!) and you would need to be physically fit. Pay is usually fairly low. It is important that you are not over sentimental with the dogs in your care — they belong to someone else and you must be able to deal with them going back to their own homes.

Some positions require you to live on site — either sharing a house, your own room in the proprietors' house, or perhaps living in a mobile home.

Training

Much of the training will be on the job. There are specific courses available, such as the Canine Studies Institute Small Animal Care Course (see page 15) and Bell Mead Training School.

Bell Mead Training School for Kennel Staff

Bell Mead Kennels (which is the country annexe of The Dogs' Home, Battersea) offers thorough training in all aspects of kennel work. The courses are open to private students or Youth Training students. Most trainees live in.

The course covers grooming, hygiene, anatomy, drugs, first aid, disease, genetics, breeding, whelping, weaning, parasites, nutrition, laws and showing.

Successful completion of the course results in the National Small Animal Care Certificate and the Bell Mead Diploma.

Contact: The Principal, Bell Mead Kennels, Priest Hill House, Priest Hill, Old Windsor, Berks SL4 2JN. Tel: Egham 432929.

Types of kennels

Boarding kennels

There are many boarding kennels across the country (details of your local ones can be found in the *Yellow Pages*). These vary enormously in size and style. Staff turnover is usually quite high as people tend to use it as a stepping stone to other things. Loyal and hard working staff are highly sought after and prized.

Quarantine kennels
When dogs are brought into this country from overseas they must stay for 6 months in a licensed quarantine kennels to ensure that they are not carrying any diseases, particularly rabies. Kennel staff may be advised by their employers to have certain inoculations to protect them from the risks of infectious diseases, such as rabies.

A list of quarantine kennels is available from:

The Ministry of Agriculture, Fisheries & Food, Great Western House, Horseferry Road, London SW1P 2AE.

Breeding/show kennels
Some breeders employ kennel staff, particularly if they own a large number of dogs. You may be looking after one breed or two or three different breeds. You may be required to prepare dogs for showing and may also attend shows, although it is more likely that you would be required to stay behind and look after the remaining dogs whilst the owner goes to the shows. You may be required to help with mating, whelping and weaning.

Summary
Vacancies may be advertised in the local press, local shop windows, in the dog press, in *Horse and Hound*, and Job Centres.

Qualities required
Stamina, physical fitness, affinity with dogs, good telephone skills, good communication skills, initiative.

- Good for experience.

- Good for gaining essential knowledge of breeds.

- Voluntary positions sometimes available.

- Part time weekend/holiday work often available.

PROFESSIONAL GROOMER

The job
As for hairdressers, there will always be a demand for grooming

services, since in most cases it is a necessity, not a luxury. Dogs will always need grooming, bathing and clipping, whatever the time of year and despite any other economic cut backs that have to be made. It is not only poodles and show dogs that need regular grooming and clipping: Spaniels, most terriers, and many other breeds need regular attention. The demand for this service is such that there are opportunities in pet shops, in veterinary surgeries, as mobile groomers, in boarding kennels and in grooming salons.

A wide variety of courses are available and it is worth taking the time to seek out reputable training schools to ensure you attain the best possible standards. Professional groomers — canine beauticians as they are often called — are all ages and from all walks of life. The courses that are available are often very flexible and can easily be fitted in around current employment.

The grooming world has its own association, the **Groomers Association**, which holds courses and annual competitions, and there are similar organisations in Europe and the USA. A City and Guilds Certificate is now available in grooming; this is a uniform qualification recognised throughout the industry.

Costs

The cost of setting up a salon or mobile service can be prohibitive, but today's equipment is very effective and, if maintained and serviced properly, will last a long time. Of course, your investment in your future is also reclaimable against tax. Secondhand equipment is often available for purchase and can be found via the weekly dog journals.

The cost of the course will vary from school to school but on average a one month course will cost you between £300 and £600. The knowledge and experience gained will last a lifetime and is an excellent string to have in your bow.

Knowledge required

Knowledge about the look of various breeds of dog is important. It is not essential to have experienced every type of breed whilst training, although the more you are familiar with the better. Individual breeds are categorised in groups (terriers, spaniels *etc*). The differences between the breeds in a particular group are not very great and once a working knowledge of the type of clip for each group has been achieved you will be able to tackle the others in the group competently using a good guide book. The *All Breed Dog Grooming Guide* by Sam Kohl and Catherine Goldstein, published by Arco, is an excellent manual, and a must for every groomer.

Handling

Handling dogs correctly whilst grooming them is vitally important. For some it will be their first time and it is very important that they go home happy so that their owners want to bring them again. Probably more importantly it will be much easier to groom a dog and keep it on the grooming table if it is relaxed and not fearful of you. Most dogs settle down extremely well, even those whose owners report that they will not allow anyone to touch them with a brush at home. Once on the grooming table dogs are usually very cooperative.

Work opportunities

Boarding kennels

For boarders in care and as an ancillary service. Helps to keep business flowing in quiet off-peak periods. Also helps to add a touch of professionalism to the business. Your clipping clients will almost certainly become boarding clients, too. The owners will be happy that their pet already knows you and they know that he knows that he goes home at the end of his visit to you.

Mobile service

Has some advantages in that the groomer does not need to pay rent to anyone. Other overheads, such as hot water and electricity are cut dramatically, if not totally. However, there are disadvantages. The dogs are often distracted by the owner to the point where grooming it properly becomes hopeless. The facilities such as the bath or sink are very often unsuitable. There is frequently too little space for a proper grooming table and the quality of lighting is likely to be variable. The time taken to travel between appointments is unpaid. More money may well be required for advertising than if you were situated in somewhere like a pet shop, for instance.

Pet shop

Clients are in ready supply and little advertising other than a notice in the shop window is required. The availability of space is important; ventilation and lighting conditions and room to keep dogs that are waiting to be clipped/collected need to be taken into account, and should not be overlooked to any degree. You are going to be spending almost all of every working day in this room, so think of how comfortable you will feel. The arrangements for rent should be clear from the start. If you are not actually employed by the pet shop owner the agreement should be put in writing. Any likely rise in rent should be noted.

Grooming salon

Employment could be found in an existing salon, or you could open your own. Suitable premises need to be found. Location is important. Salons off the beaten track will never be as popular as salons that are convenient to get to, bearing in mind that the owner needs to be able to drop the dog off and return sometime later to collect it. If you are situated in an out of the way place one way round the problem is to offer a collection/delivery service, although this also has its disadvantages in running costs and more importantly in the time spent driving when you could be clipping.

Equipment needed

Here is a list of basic equipment that you will need and the approximate cost:

Free standing dryer	£ 299.00
Adjustable table	£ 530.00
Clippers	£ 120.00
Blades	£ 75.00
Combs	£ 15.00
Brushes	£ 12.00
Scissors	£ 50.00
Thinning scissors	£ 35.00
Stripping knife	£ 12.00
Nail clippers	£ 6.00
	£1154.00

Add to this list a bath with shower attachments, towels, washing and drying facilities for towels, shampoos and some kind of indoor kennel arrangement for holding dogs that have been, or are waiting to be, clipped. In your own premises rent or mortgage costs must also be taken into consideration, as must electricity, telephone and water rates.

Useful addresses

The Groomers Association
Bedford Business Centre
170 Mile Road
Bedford
MK42 9TW
Tel: (01234) 273933

Paws Awhile
3b Ashley Road
Southport
Merseyside
PR9 0RB
Tel: (01704) 44519

Canine Comforts Ltd
International Grooming School
6 Green Parade
Whitten Road
Hounslow
Essex
TW13 2BN
Tel: (0181) 894 2999

Paws and Claws
298 Prince Avenue
Westcliffe On Sea
Essex
SS0 0NF
Tel: (01702) 431833

A day in the life of . . .

Ann Brocklehurst, Top Dog Grooming Services, Leamington Spa

'Before I became a professional groomer I ran a restaurant but what I really wanted to do was to work with dogs in some way. I decided to become a groomer when I began showing one of my own dogs and had to learn how to prepare its coat for the ring. I quickly realised that grooming was a skill that could be developed into a business and it would also mean that I could work for myself. I went on a very intensive two week course and developed my general dog handling skills at the local dog club. I began on a part-time basis until I had built up my confidence (and my client base). I will always remember my first client was a shaggy mongrel that the owner wanted clipped to look like a poodle! To get started I managed to buy clippers and some other larger pieces of equipment second hand through an advert in the local paper. I placed my own advertisements in pet shops, local veterinary surgeries and in local papers. Today, I don't have to advertise at all as my clients come to me on recommendation.

'Although my work keeps me busy all the year round, the summer months are particularly hectic. I groom, on average, five dogs per day. I particularly enjoy hand stripping even though it takes longer than clipping but the end result is very pleasing.

'I run a collection and delivery service, which means I have to collect the dogs at 7.30am, because I start clipping at 8am, and drop them off after 5pm, when I finish. That means that some dogs stay with me all day, which is quite useful as I can work on them around the ones brought in by the owners and that are only with me for a couple of hours.

'I am based at home. I converted the garage into a grooming parlour and it is now fitted with a bath, heating, and good lights. I find it much better working from home. When I first started I ran a mobile service but I found that I spent too much time driving around and carrying my equipment in and out of people's houses. More importantly, I found that the dogs behave much better away from their owners and home environment, which makes the whole experience much more pleasant for me and the dog.

'As a large amount of my time is spent bathing and drying dogs when I get very busy I sometimes get someone in who can help in this department.

'There is, of course, always plenty of cleaning up to do — dog hair seems to get in everywhere! The clippers and other equipment all needs to be sterilised regularly, too.

'In my job you are dealing hands on with dogs all the time, so a good knowledge of them, and handling skills, are very important. I also think that people skills are very important; I see most of my clients regularly and so it's inevitable that I get to know some of them very well. You become very much part of their lives, particularly the elderly, and I think it's very important to them to see you as a pleasant, approachable, trustworthy person who cares about their companion.'

DOG WARDENS

The job
The 1992 Environmental Protection Act stated that all local authorities must employ an officer responsible for the collection of stray dogs. Some local authorities put the service out to tender and some employ staff direct.

The job function differs from region to region depending on the particular local authority, their attitude to dogs, the local area and the staff involved. The following is based on the Dog Warden Service at Leicester City Council. It is a particularly forward thinking and innovative department and, despite regional differences, should provide a good insight into the profession.

The Leicester Dog Warden team consists of:

1. Senior Dog Warden (or Team Leader) — who is responsible for the day to day running of the department. The Senior Dog Warden is answerable to a Group Manager in the Environmental Health Department. It is the Group Manager who would make long term policy and financial decisions.

2. Dog Wardens
    The role of the dog warden is twofold:

    — Reactive, for example dealing with complaints about strays, noise, fouling, general nuisance. Whenever possible dog wardens try to alleviate the problems caused by irresponsible ownership.

— Pro-active, for example the promotion of responsible dog ownership and campaign work, trying to get people more interested by working on a broader scope with subliminal messages such as a 'Dogs are Good for People' campaign.

Qualifications

Leicester City Council works on a non-academic footing, although applicants must be literate and numerate. Good written skills are important as there is a lot of paper work. A driving licence is essential.

Qualities required

Experience with people is very important as there is a lot of cold calling — knocking on doors not knowing what response you are going to receive. Communication skills are also important as you would be required to meet and give talks to the general public.

A sense of humour is vital, as a stress reliever amongst other things. You must be a team worker, be able to use your initiative and think on your feet in awkward and stressful situations, for example, at the scene of a road traffic accident where a dog may be involved. Although you may be part of a team much of the working day is spent alone and you must be comfortable with that.

When the last vacancy for a dog warden arose in Leicester it was advertised in the local press and 250 applications were received, so good application skills were essential to avoid being disregarded at the first stage.

Training

Many weeks will be spent with experienced members of the team until you are ready to work alone. At Leicester, time is also spent at the RSPCA kennels so that trainee wardens get a good overview of the situation. Similarly, a day is spent with the RSPCA Inspectors so that wardens become aware of the difference between the role of the Inspector and a dog warden, as dog wardens do not deal with cases of cruelty and neglect. Dog wardens are also sent to relevant external courses, for example seminars on behaviour, and have in-house courses on writing skills, media presentation, public speaking and other topics.

It is important that dog wardens build up their general knowledge about dogs and their behaviour. Although they do not give in-depth advice on specific problems, they must be able to provide general guidance.

Vacancies

Part time possibilities: some city councils, as with Leicester, have a job share scheme and some of the contracted-in wardens around the country are part time.

Work experience placements are possible.

Vacancies are announced in the local press and local authority newsletters.

Contact: your local Environmental Health Department. Do not send applications on spec, but it may be worth enquiring to see what experience may be useful.

National Dog Warden Association

NDWA was founded by a number of active dog wardens who wished to share their experiences with others in the profession. It is now able to offer advice and problem solving to fellow dog wardens, promote education, use publicity and promotion to further its goals, and help with the training of personnel. The NDWA runs seminars, dog handling courses and individual training.

A leaflet entitled *Guidance Notes for those considering a career as a Dog Warden* is available from the NDWA, c/o Mr D Griffiths, Environmental Health Department, East Hampshire District Council, Penns Place, Petersfield, Hants. Tel: (01730) 266551 or Mrs Sue Bell (01684) 295010 (Chairman).

A day in the life of . . . .

Geraldine Fleming, Leicester City Council Dog Warden
'We usually start work at around 9am (we work on a flexi-time basis). My first task is to go through the complaints, prioritise and deal with them accordingly. We have a council charter whereby we have guaranteed response times — immediate response in the case of dangerous dogs complaints, as soon as practical for strays, and three days in the case of complaints of noise, fouling and nuisance. As Team Leader it is my responsibility to ensure that these times are met. To help facilitate this we are all in radio contact throughout the day.

'Stray dogs that we pick up are taken to the RSPCA kennels. We are very lucky in that we have a very close relationship with the RSPCA. The three of us bring in an average of fifteen dogs each per month.

'I have huge amounts of paperwork to do — all stages of a complaint are recorded; the complainant and dog owner are fully notified at each stage of the complaint.

'I also have to find time for meetings, both within the department and with some outside organisations. For example, I have to attend Tenants Associations Meetings if there is a dog issue on the agenda.

'We try to have a team meeting once a week. Since we spend a lot of time on our own it's a chance to get together and see if anything needs altering or if anyone's got any ideas about campaigns etc.

'Since I started as a Dog Warden 10 years ago, the service and training have changed beyond recognition. We like to try as far as possible to keep away from the traditional dog catcher image. Consequently I get a lot of satisfaction from our promotional campaigns. Ideally I would like lots more time to spend on this to make a big impact on the City and to prevent the problems arising — I would like to see the service approached in a holistic sense. Certainly people's attitudes have changed following our recent ''Dogs are Good for People'' campaign.

'The best bits of the job are the happy endings — genuinely lost dogs being reunited with their owners. The positive feed back from our campaigns is also a motivator — people start to see us as a resource for information.

'The worst bits are the relentless problems that seem never ending. There will always be strays and fouling. The enormity of the problem is quite staggering. It doesn't help that people tend to have an unrealistic expectation of what we can do for them. Sadly there are still a huge number of dogs being put down every day — in the end it's always the dog that pays the price.

'Some days we have to monitor noisy dogs by sitting outside their houses and recording how long a dog is barking for. This can then be used as evidence in court if necessary if a prosecution has to be made.

'Some days are taken up with talks to schools and other organisations. We do not go in and lecture on responsible dog ownership, but we try to push across that message with Prevent-a-Bite talks and explain how dogs help people in society.

'There are some out of hours duties, such as evening talks and I often end up taking paperwork home to get it finished.'

Editor's note

A NCDL survey in 1993 showed that nationally the problem of

strays and unwanted dogs had gone up. In Leicester however, the problem has gone down and credit must be given to the enthusiasm and skill of the dog wardens in that area.

VETERINARY NURSING

The job
Veterinary nurses work alongside veterinary surgeons caring for sick and injured animals. Their work includes: theatre work (including anaesthesia), cleaning, instrument sterilisation, assistance in consultation rooms, ordering drugs, radiography, laboratory diagnostic tests, caring for in-patients and telephone/reception duties. In addition they may be involved in pet health counselling, puppy socialisation parties, enhancing client/practice relations, or dealing with company reps.

Training
Applicants must be aged 17 or over and have 4 GCSEs including English Language, Science and/or Maths. The applicants work at approved training centres for the full two year duration of the course (a list of training centres is available from BVNA for £2.00). Theoretical training may be at the centre, at a college or by correspondence course through the Canine Studies Institute (see page 15). Some colleges offer a 6 month 'block' course.

The first year of training covers basic nursing, anatomy, physiology and leads to the Part One examination. In the second year surgical, medical & special nursing, radiography and laboratory work are covered culminating in the Part Two examination. After passing both exams your name would be entered on the Register of qualified Veterinary Nurses and you would be entitled to use the letters VN after your name.

British Veterinary Nursing Association (BNVA)
The BNVA was founded in 1965 and membership is open to all students, veterinary nurses and practice staff. It aims to promote a high standard of veterinary nursing and to improve the status and conditions for veterinary nurses.

The BVNA runs branch meetings, refresher courses, an annual Congress and publishes a bi-monthly journal. It also operates an employment register.

Details can be obtained from the BVNA (enclose a stamped addressed envelope):

BVNA Office
Unit 12D The Seedbed Centre
Coldharbour Road, Harlow
Essex CM19 5AF.

Opportunities for veterinary nurses

Apart from working in veterinary practices, there are also possibilities of employment in research establishments, laboratories, universities, colleges, zoos, nature reserves, pharmaceutical companies, breeding/boarding kennels, lecturing, and welfare organisations.

There are also opportunities in other areas, for example pet food manufacturers' sales teams.

The above section on Veterinary Nursing has been approved by and reproduced with the kind permission of the BVNA. A leaflet entitled *General Information — Veterinary Nursing* is available from the BVNA at the above address on receipt of a large SAE. Information has also been drawn from the Blue Cross leaflet, *Working With Animals — Veterinary Nursing*, available from the Blue Cross.

The BVNA have also produced a good video entitled *Veterinary Nursing — Is this the career for you?* Details as above.

Pet health counselling

The Pet Health Counselling course is run by Pedigree Petfoods and the training is open to veterinary nurses and practice staff with at least three years' experience. The students attend a three or four day course, learning about how to give advice on:

- preventive medicine
- pet selection
- nutrition
- pet insurance
- pet accessories
- bereavement counselling.

Also, how to run clinics on:
- obesity
- ageing
- training & behaviour
- oral hygiene.

A Pet Health Counsellor Co-ordinator provides back up, both on a personal basis and in the Pet Health Counsellor's newsletter.

Further details from: Pet Health Counsellor Co-ordinator, Pedigree Petfoods National Office, Waltham on the Wolds, Melton Mowbray, Leicestershire LE14 4RS.

A day in the life of . . . .

Terri Plaister, Head Nurse, John Speer's Veterinary Surgery, Birmingham

'I had always wanted to work with animals and after doing a two week work experience placement when I was at school I decided to go into veterinary nursing. Fortunately the practice where I did my work experience immediately offered me a part time job, doing reception work and cleaning, during weekends. When I eventually left school I went on to work there full time.

'I moved to my present practice when I started my VN training as this surgery is registered as an approved training centre. I have now worked my way up to Head Nurse, in charge of two other nurses and a junior, who looks after the kennels.

'We do weekly shifts, working either 9am - 5pm, 1pm - 8pm or 8am - 1pm, and take it in turns to provide weekend cover.

'My usual morning routine finds me assisting in the operating theatre between 9am and 1pm. I have recently completed my training as a pet health counsellor which means that I can now advise clients on diet, worming, fleas, behaviour and provide some bereavement counselling. In my role as the pet health counsellor I am often called away from my usual duties to talk to clients, but the receptionists usually try to make appointments for clients to see me when they know I'm going to be available. In the afternoons I might work in the laboratory, follow up on anything from the morning theatre, order drugs or deal with company reps.

'In my own time I run puppy parties. These are great fun and are meant to help socialise puppies and get them used to other people, other dogs, the veterinary surgery and so on. The parties take place between the puppy's first and second set of vaccinations — when they return for their second jab you can easily tell which puppies have been to the party as they look so happy to be here! I also run an obesity clinic for overweight animals and a Well Animal clinic, which is for older dogs.

'Sometimes I have to do some rather unexpected jobs, such as speaking on the local radio when Mr Speer, the senior partner in the practice, does his monthly radio show. I am often called upon to give comments on new products, etc.

'The parts of my job I like best are talking to clients, watching animals that have recovered from being very sick being reunited with their owners — the moment when they see each other is very special and I feel privileged to witness it. I also enjoy working in the operating theatre and seeing the wonderful relationship some owners have with their pets.

'The worst bits are the cleaning and putting animals to sleep. (Happily, at this practice we will not put healthy animals to sleep; we will try to do all we can to find them another home rather than do that.) Counselling bereaved owners can be very stressful and I have to guard against becoming too involved.

'I think that anyone has to be truly dedicated to want to do this job. It is possible to make a career structure for yourself as there are plenty of opportunities to do things, but you really need the initiative and confidence to find out what is there and what will suit you.'

VETERINARY SURGEON

The job
Veterinary surgeons in general practice work on diagnosis and treatment of disease and injury, inoculation against disease and advice on diet and breeding. In small animal practice the veterinary surgeon would be dealing with pet and domestic animals. Large animal practices also deal with farm animals such as horses and cows, and some veterinary surgeons deal with exotic animals. Companion animal practices are also becoming popular; these deal with pet and domestic animals and horses.

Veterinary surgeons are employed not only in private practice, but by the Royal Army Veterinary Corps, research institutions, pharmaceutical companies, in teaching, animal welfare organisations and in local government (supervising the enforcement of public health and animal welfare legislation).

As well as possessing other skills, applicants need to be academically very capable. The work can be physically demanding (particularly in large animal practice) and requires a dedication to animals and good business skills. Communication skills are also important as a veterinary surgeon will be dealing with pet owners as much as with the pets themselves.

Most veterinary surgeons begin their careers as assistants in a practice and may later become a partner (this requires financial investment into the practice). Most veterinary surgeons in private practice are self employed (apart from assistants).

Qualifications

3 A-levels with high grades for entry into one of the six university veterinary schools — Bristol, Cambridge, Edinburgh, Glasgow, Liverpool and London. The course will last either five or six years, depending on the university. A few applications from mature students are considered each year — these applicants need to have a 1st or upper 2nd class honours degree in a related subject, such as biochemistry or zoology. The veterinary degree obtained allows the vet to become a member of the Royal College of Veterinary Surgeons. Only members of the RCVS are allowed to practise.

The course covers scientific disciplines, dealing with animal structure and functions, pharmacology, pathology, microbiology, parasitology and bacteriology, animal health, husbandry, clinical medicine and surgery, reproduction and veterinary public health. During the vacation periods students are required to obtain relevant experience.

Royal College of Veterinary Surgeons

The RCVS is the professional governing body of veterinary surgeons. It sets the academic standards for all of the teaching colleges as well as setting professional standards.

Royal College of Veterinary Surgeons
32 Belgrave Square
London SW1X 8QP.

British Small Animal Veterinary Association

The BSAVA represents veterinary surgeons in small animal practice and publishes a number of veterinary related books as well as running courses, talks and an Annual Congress for Veterinary Surgeons.

BSAVA
Kingsley House
Church Lane
Shurdington
Cheltenham
Glos GL51 5TQ.
Tel: (01242) 862994

British Veterinary Association

The BVA is an umbrella organisation overseeing the other groups, such as BSAVA. It publishes the *Vet Record*, a weekly journal, and also runs an Annual Congress.

British Veterinary Association
7 Mansfield Street
London
W1M 0AT

A day in the life of . . .

David Bell BVetMed Cert SAO MRCVS, The Scarsdale Veterinary Hospital, Derby

'I qualified as a Veterinary Surgeon in 1977 from the Royal Veterinary College in London. After qualification I stayed on there as a house surgeon for two years and then spent another six months in the medicine department. In 1979 I joined my present practice as an assistant and five years later became a partner.

'I decided to go into the veterinary profession because I wanted to do something biologically based and liked the potential variety of the job. I pictured a veterinary surgeon being out and about more than GPs, for example, plus being able to carry out X-rays, do laboratory work and surgery in addition to consulting.

'I find it a very rewarding job and although I very much enjoy working with people and consulting, I particularly enjoy surgery. I have a Certificate in Small Animal Orthopaedics, a postgraduate qualification which means that I am able to offer a referral service to veterinary surgeons from other practices, so 2.5 days of my working week are spent operating, unless a client particularly wishes to see me.

'We have a large practice here, employing over 40 staff, some of whom are part time. The practice is split into large animal and small animal units, with seven veterinary surgeons on both sides. Our main small animal surgery has hospital status and we have two additional branch surgeries.

'There are some unpleasant aspects to the job. Sometimes putting an animal to sleep can be quite distressing, especially if the owner is very emotional — I'm sure you can imagine the very real sadness of having to put an elderly lady's dog to sleep when it may be the last real link she had with her late husband. The general public can cause distress occasionally, even though the vast majority are charming. In all walks of life you always get the ones who will complain about anything, even though they may be quite unjustified.

'We are often required to work long and unsociable hours. In our practice the small animal vets are on duty one in every five weekends. Another one in five of those weekends we are also on stand-by. During the week evening duties are carried out on a rota system.

We try to work as much as possible on a fixed day-time rota system, aiming to have the same vets in the same locations each week, which is preferable for continuity. All duties are shared equally by all staff, whether assistants or senior partners.'

PROFESSIONAL DOG TRAINER

The job
Professional dog trainers work in a variety of locations doing all kinds of jobs. This section is primarily concerned with dog trainers who train pet dogs and their owners, but there are also greyhound racing trainers, gun dog trainers, sheep dog trainers and security dog trainers many of whom are attached to a specific kennels. A list of useful addresses follows at the end of this section.

Professional pet dog trainers differ from individuals who run dog training clubs as a hobby and only charge a nominal fee to cover the cost of the room hire. Professionals may run private dog training classes, puppy socialisation classes or offer individual lessons. In some circumstances they may take dogs into their own premises for training, but it is important, if this is done, that training of the owner is not neglected.

Many professional dog trainers are self employed and may work full or part time. Transport is essential so that the trainer can reach particular training areas and clients' homes if training is to be carried out in that location.

Pet dog trainers train dogs to respond to control commands, such as come, heel, sit, down, stay. Ideally dog trainers should also encourage responsible dog ownership, for example not allowing the dogs to foul public places and encouraging owners to clear up after them if they do.

Many trainers may start their education in local dog clubs where they gain experience in teaching all kinds of people and types of dogs. Some are retired from other professions, such as police dog handlers.

The ability to communicate well with owners is just as important as communication with the dogs. Trainers must be able to empathise with those owners who may be disappointed that their pet has not responded to their attempts to train it and try to help them achieve realistic training objectives.

Trainers also need to be able to differentiate between training problems and behavioural problems that obedience training will not correct and which need to be treated by a behavioural counsellor.

There are numerous courses at all levels which provide dog trainers with the knowledge they require to be able to teach the most effective and kindest methods of training. These are generally advertised in the weekly dog journals, *Our Dogs*, *Dog World* and *Dog Training Weekly* and *Obedience Competitor*.

Courses

The **Association of Pet Dog Trainers** was set up to promote kind methods of training with dog clubs. Obtain details from: APDT, Greengarth, Maddox Lane, Bookham, Surrey KT23 3HT.

The **British Institute for Professional Dog Trainers** runs courses throughout the country. Courses range from a Certificate of Basic Instructional Techniques to an Advanced Certificate in Techniques of Training, Instructing, Administration and Organisation. Details from: Tom Buckley (General Secretary), Bowstone Gate, Nr Disley, Cheshire. Tel: (016637) 62772.

Anglo American Dog Training: Roy Hunter organises weekly residential, weekend and day courses as well as evening talks and Fun Days. Details from Roy Hunter, Anglo American Dog Training, Abelard, Dyers End, Stambourne, Halstead, Essex CO9 4NE. Tel: (01440 085) 720.

Dr Ian Dunbar: videos and books on dog training, behaviour and puppy classes. c/o Carole Duke, James & Kenneth Publishers, PO Box 440, Kings Langley, Herts.

John Rogerson courses — training, behaviour and working trials courses at all levels. PO Box 4, Thirsk, North Yorkshire YO7 3YR.

The National Greyhound Racing Club, 24-28 Oval Road, London NW1 7DA.

International Sheep Dog Society, Secretary, Chesham House, 47 Bromham Road, Bedford MK40 2AA. This is the governing body for registration of border collies and administrators and organisers of the National and International Sheep Dog Trials.

Agricultural Training Board, 32-34 Beckenham Road, Kent. Has training officers based throughout the country who organise courses for sheep dog training.

A day in the life of . . .

Marie Miller, Paws 'N' Learn Puppy Training, Coventry
'I have owned dogs for over 16 years and got bitten by the bug of dog training when I began to train my own dogs. I joined a local dog club and eventually became an instructor there. However, I was mortified when my own dog, Jodie, began to display serious beha-

vioural problems. I had a consultation with David Appleby, a pet behaviour counsellor, who explained to me what had gone wrong. It was clear to him that Jodie had not been properly socialised as a puppy. This, to me, was like Pandora's Box opening; I realised how important this is for puppies and set about arranging puppy socialisation classes. At that time many dog clubs could not accept puppies until they were six months old so I decided to start private classes. Initially I worked on the project with two other trainers and then a year later launched ''Paws 'N' Learn'' on my own. It has been running successfully for four years now.

'Before I started, I attended a number of lectures and courses, including a specialised two day course with David which specifically covered puppy training and socialisation. I also did a lot of reading, and armed with the hands-on experience that I had already gained at the dog club and with my own dogs, I felt ready to help the public.

'I now run a ''baby'' puppy class, and an intermediate class which is for any dogs too old to join the puppy class. We also have an adult social group, which is for the people who just want to keep on coming! It is purely for pet dogs; we teach acceptable social behaviour, how to develop the right relationship and have fun with a dog. I have classes in Hinckley and in Coventry. In Hinckley the classes share a venue with another private club. After moving on from the puppy classes they can go on to the other club for further training. I also run a working trials night for a local club, where a group of us get together to share ideas and experiences.

'One of the problems I encountered in setting up my business was finding a venue where dogs are allowed. Anywhere where there is a nursery class or where food is prepared will not allow it. Scouts groups or others who have to fund their own facilities are often very helpful, as can be the local council.

'Helping out at a dog club can be a good training ground for dog trainers. They can learn how to deal with people and how to instruct, as well as experiencing lots of dogs with different temperaments. Practical experience to my mind is essential. Some clubs have junior sections for educating the younger handlers and my 13 year old son has recently joined another dog club as I feel that it is important for him to see other people's training techniques. I want him to learn from others as well as myself so that he can make his own decisions about the training of his first dog.

'A vital ingredient is putting your knowledge across successfully, so people skills are as important as the ability to handle dogs. You must be able to give people the confidence to handle their dog and to be able to motivate them to put the techniques into practice. They must not be made to feel silly or that their dog is a hopeless case. I can't count the number of times I have seen an instructor take a dog from its owners, make it do a task it would not do for them and then hand it back, making it look as if previous failure was entirely the owner's fault. This is very sad and does not help anyone.

'Most people require lessons in the evenings or at weekends, so that dictates when I run my classes. I have to be prepared to make that time commitment.

'I really enjoy training the puppies. It's satisfying to see them socialise well with people, children and other dogs. I can also identify those who are going to grow up to be problems, despite being socialised. I can make the owner aware of what they've got and explain how to prevent the problem from developing further so that they don't end up with a maniac on a lead.

'When people phone me I always check their motives for wanting to come to a class. If it is not a puppy, what is it they want to change in their dog? This way I can weed out the behavioural problems, which my classes would be inappropriate for, and pass them onto David, who has a behavioural clinic in my area.

'My sort of professional dog training, and the scale on which I choose to operate, is not financially rewarding. People are less willing to pay for preventative advice even though it will help them in the future. However, Paws 'N' Learn is self financing, supplements my own dog training activities and satisfies my interest.'

PET BEHAVIOUR COUNSELLORS

The job
The role of the behaviour counsellor is to advise owners whose dogs have developed inappropriate behaviour. This is different from standard obedience training offered by professional dog trainers. Behavioural problems include such things as aggression towards people, dogs or other animals, destructiveness, toileting problems, inappropriate vocal behaviour and phobias.

Bona fide pet behavioural counsellors work strictly on referral from veterinary surgeons. Where necessary there will be close liaison between the counsellor and the referring veterinary surgeon. Pet behaviour counselling covers a huge variety of aspects of animal ethology, biology and human psychology.

Qualifications

There are, at time of going to press, no specific qualifications to become a behaviour counsellor. However the **Association of Pet Behaviour Counsellors**, an international network of experienced behavioural counsellors, has set strict criteria for membership and a code of conduct.

A course has recently been introduced by the Anthrozoology Institute, University of Southampton, entitled the 'Certificate of Advanced Studies: Companion Animal Behaviour Counselling'. It covers cats, small mammals and horses as well as dogs, and results in an academic qualification recognised by the APBC and other professional bodies. Normal entry requirements are suitable experience and a degree or other approved qualification. Further details are available from the Department of Adult Continuing Education, Highfield, Southampton SO17 1BJ. Tel: (01703) 593469.

Courses

Courses and lectures on canine behaviour are run regularly all over the country by various organisations. They are usually advertised in the weekly dog journals, *Our Dogs*, *Dog World* and *Dog Training Weekly*. Some talks and courses will be 'interest only'; others are more advanced. They do not result in an academically recognised qualification, though some issue a certificate of attendance, but they will certainly help you to gain vital knowledge and keep you up to date with the latest findings. One useful course is the Canine Studies Institute Human/Animal Interface correspondence course which gives a good introduction to canine behaviour. See page 15 for details.

The APBC run an annual symposium which brings together prominent speakers in the field and up to date findings. To be put on the mailing list for details of the Symposium please write to the APBC at the address below.

Qualities needed

A training in biology, ethology, psychology or veterinary science is preferred. Good counselling skills and an empathy with people are essential, plus a good all round knowledge of animal and human behaviour and the ability to put across information in a way the client can comprehend and implement.

A large amount of paperwork is involved, for example, writing reports to referring veterinary surgeons and clients. There is also much communication by telephone, so good administration skills are important.

Most behavioural counsellors are self employed.

Contact

APBC, 257 Royal College Street, London NW1.

Symposium details, book and product list, list of members/ practices.

A day in the life of . . .

David Appleby MAPBC, Pet Behaviour Counsellor

'My job as a pet behaviour counsellor causes me to travel a lot. I have nine regular clinics around the Midlands in veterinary hospitals, PDSA and RSPCA clinics as well as Cambridge University Veterinary School. I also consult at the Pet Behaviour Centre in Worcestershire where I am based.

'On a full clinic day I may see five or six clients, all on referral from their veterinary surgeons. I spend about an hour and a half with each of them, taking a detailed history of the problem and discussing how best to modify their dog or cat's behaviour. After the consultation I remain in telephone contact with my clients for updates, progress reports and where necessary to modify advice in light of the dog or cat's response to the behaviour modification programme. I always plan to be in my office every Monday so that clients and vets know that they can reach me on that day, so that day is always spent almost entirely on the telephone. On other days the phone is always manned in office hours and I am contactable if necessary.

'The success of behaviour modification very much depends upon the owner's compliance in carrying out the modification programme. Unfortunately a few clients wish you to wave a magic wand and make everything better, but it doesn't work like that. Although in some instances very rapid progress can be made, more often a thorough and systematic approach has to be taken which can be time consuming and involves all members of the family. It is extremely satisfying to see a family enjoying their dog again instead of it just causing them stress.

'As well as consulting I give talks and lectures to interested parties, which I particularly enjoy. They include monthly talks at an RSPCA and a NCDL animal home to the owners of newly acquired dogs. This helps ensure that they get off to the best possible start in their new relationship with each other by avoiding the development of behavioural problems.

'Of course, I also attend other people's talks and lectures, and within the APBC we have regular education days so that all members are kept up to date with the latest developments in the field of behavioural therapy. My role as practice representative within the

APBC entails collating an annual report of cases seen by APBC members.

'I also spend quite a lot of time writing, both articles for the canine press and a series of booklets that we publish ourselves and distribute to veterinary surgeries, dog clubs etc. The booklets currently available are based on how to prevent behaviour problems developing (*How To Have a Happy Puppy*), how to establish general control over your dog (*The Good Behaviour Guide*), as well as *The Behavioural Effects of Canine Castration*, written by Hazel Palmer, an APBC colleague, and edited by myself.'

SEARCH AND RESCUE DOG ASSOCIATION

The job

SARDA was founded in Scotland in 1965 and initially covered the whole of Britain. In 1971 it was divided into Scottish, English and Welsh Associations. There are SARDAs in the Highlands, South Scotland, England, England Lake District, Wales and Ireland. The following feature is based on SARDA Wales.

The function of SARDA dogs and handlers is to help expedite the rescue of people missing on the hills, to help save lives and minimise pain and suffering to anyone stranded in remote areas. On a search in winter conditions the rescue dog is equal to at least 20 human searchers. SARDA handlers also assist local police forces in searching for missing people, anywhere.

All handlers are volunteers who pay for the maintenance of their dogs, rescue equipment and travelling expenses. All handlers are competent mountaineers who must be active members of a mountain rescue team and their services are called upon on average around 40 times per year.

The dog works by picking up the air scent of missing persons, following the scent to its source and then returning to the handler to indicate the find. Every 24 to 36 hours humans lose a layer of skin; these microscopic particles are called 'rafts' and are carried on the wind. The dog works with its nose up, and when it comes across an air-scent 'cone' it will turn into it and follow it to its source, which will typically be a body or an article of clothing from the person.

Most dogs used are border collies but German shepherd dogs and labradors are also used. The teams work in mountainous terrains and open wilderness areas often in the worst of weather conditions. The dogs have to be trained to be winched in and out of helicopters as it is frequently not possible to land a helicopter in the mountains. In fact, things that most people would consider to be rather strange are normal to a SARDA dog.

The handler owns, lives with and trains his own dog which he will have obtained at 8 weeks of age. Its first assessment will be between 2 and 3 years of age, depending on the dog's maturity. Assessments are over a period of 3 or 4 days. Having passed the first assessment the dog will be called a 'novice search dog'. After a further year there is a second assessment and having passed the dog will be called a 'full search dog'. All being well the dog and handler will then only be brought forward for assessment every three years for the purpose of regrade and confirming maintenance of standards.

Training and support
Throughout the year there will also be official training sessions, lectures and discussions on various aspects of search work, such as the effect of wind and terrain on scent, or organising the search.

SARDA is supported by Friends who raise money for the charity and also provide 'bodies' to aid the training of the dogs. These are volunteers who hide themselves on the side of a mountain in all sorts of weather conditions and stay there until they are found by one of the dogs. SARDA Wales also receives support from Pedigree Petfoods.

Contact
SARDA Wales, Jed Stone (Hon. Secretary), 15 Maes-Y-Braich, Dolwyddelan, Gwynedd LL25 0YQ.

I ORIGINALLY WANTED TO WORK THE SKI SLOPES

3
Service Careers

If you would like to combine working with dogs with a career in the services, perhaps in uniform, these are some of the careers which could be open to you:

- police dog handler
- prison officer dog handler
- drug detection dogs (Customs & Excise)
- British Transport police dog handler
- Royal Army Veterinary Corps
- Royal Air Force

POLICE DOG HANDLER

The job

The police dog handler is a support service for the uniformed officers and their role depends largely on the environment within which they are working. The emphasis varies in terms of deployment and training. For example, in mountainous areas tracking will have a priority; in inner city areas it may not be as important.

The basic objectives are:

- preventative and operational patrols
- tracking
- searching
- recovery of articles at scenes of crime
- locating children and missing persons
- deterring rowdyism.

The Home Office Standing Advisory Committee on Police Dogs advises on how all police dogs are trained, the minimum standards and how dogs should be deployed. The Home Office manual, *Police Dogs Training & Care*, is followed by all the dog schools.

Organisation

Nationally, the police service is divided into regions which, in turn, are divided into forces. There are 9 Regional Police Dog Training Schools which are centres of excellence. Each force also has its own training centre to which operational stations report. Individual forces either train their dogs and handlers at their own force training centre or send them to their regional school for a 13 week residential training course.

The dogs

There are 2,243 working police dogs (May 94) of which over 1,700 are German shepherd dogs. The majority of the remainder are labradors or springer spaniels used for explosive and firearms detection.

Dogs are either donated by the public or may be bought in from kennels or breeders. The donated dogs must be under two years of age (to ensure the best value from the dog as a police dog it will be retired at about six or seven years of age). All animals are entire and dogs are preferred to bitches. German shepherd dogs are normally used as police dogs. They have not only proved to be the best all round breed for the task, they have also become accepted by the public as police dogs. Donated dogs are assessed in the home environment and then brought into the force training centre for further assessment. If considered suitable, the dog will be matched with a handler. Experienced handlers may run a new dog alongside their already operational dog whilst the handler is building up its responses and drive for tracking and searching. The dog is then introduced to formal obedience before starting the 13 week training course. During their working lives police dogs live at home with the handlers. On retirement, a dog will often be retained as a family pet by its handler.

Training

Following the thirteen week training course at the regional centre, continuation training develops and builds on the skills learned during the course and continues throughout the dog's working life. For example, during the course the dogs will be trained to track on a soft surface; during the continuation training the dog will be taught to track on hard surfaces also.

Recruitment

On average, prospective officers will have completed six or seven years in the force and will have applied as a result of an internal circulation. The candidate is then assessed on his/her police skills, sickness record, the stability of his/her home environment, whether the applicant has a garden large enough for a kennel and facilities to transport the dog to and from work. The officer's application must also be supported by their line management.

Depending on local procedure suitable applicants are selected for interview before a board. This is followed by a two week assessment course which includes a physical fitness assessment. If the applicant is still interested and considered suitable he/she will be offered a position within the following 12 months and in the meantime returns to their previous post.

Tenure of post

To encourage a turnover of staff, specialist roles generally within the police force are for a limited time period only, after which the police officer will return to main stream policing. The length of the posting to the dog section will be dependent upon the working life of their dog, ie 5-6 years. Provided the officer has given good service and wishes to remain on the section, he/she may be offered the opportunity to work a second dog, although this does vary with local procedures. At the end of the second dog's working life the officer may return to other duties.

There are male and female dog handlers, all of whom work shifts.

Grades

Police Dog Handler   — Constable
                     — Sergeant
                     — Inspector

The job can be very varied, from patrolling football matches to doing PR work, talks to local schools etc. In-Service Dog Trials are held every year held in conjunction with agricultural shows. There are also the National Police Dog Trials which culminate in 30 officers competing for the Police Dog of the Year award, having first qualified at a regional level.

Working with explosive search dogs

During the late 1970s the German shepherd dog's strong search instinct was utilised in the search for explosives. Initially the dogs were trained for all of the tasks but it was felt that it was unfair to expect the dogs to search for people and property and then for arms and explosives whilst ignoring the former, so dual task dogs were phased out and specialist dogs introduced. Other breeds were also introduced which displayed a strong retrieve instinct. Every force now has a number of explosive search dogs all of which are trained at the regional training schools.

The explosive search dog searches venues prior to organised visits by dignitaries. They also search and clear buildings where reported devices have been left. Some experienced handlers may work both a patrol dog and an explosive search dog, which is a huge time commitment both at work and at home.

In all police dog work, a high degree of obedience is required, but this is especially important with explosive search dogs. You would not really want an unexploded device being brought back and dropped into your hands!

Working with drugs dogs
The Drug Squad also have dogs trained in the detection of drugs; these are a separate section to the patrol dogs.

Entering the Police Force
Minimum age: 18yrs 3mths
Maximum age: 55 yrs

Applicants must be in good physical condition and be able to speak English. There are no minimum academic qualifications but the applicant will take a standard entrance test. The applicant must have no criminal record.

It can take around 6 months from date of the applicant applying to getting into the force.

There are some graduate placement schemes (similar to work experience) — details can be obtained from your Regional Headquarters.

Details of local recruitment can be obtained from your Regional Headquarters.

A day in the life of . . .
Sergeant Steve Lewis, Dog Handler, West Midlands Police
'I have been in the Force for 29 years, 25 of which have been on the Dog Section. These days it would not be possible to stay on one section for so long due to the tenure of post policy, but as I am due to retire when my present dog does I should not be affected. Before I joined the Force I was a lorry driver — I had two pet dogs who travelled extensively with me, but I had not had any experience of actually working with dogs. Within 18 months of joining the Police Force, however, I knew that I wanted to be a

dog handler. I had a good record of achievement since joining which helped my case and was fortunate in being successful on my first application.

'I have had three dogs in all (all German Shepherds), Triton, Sonny and Dusty, my present dog. I kept Triton and Sonny as pets after their retirement, as I will Dusty.

'We work a ''rolling'' shift system, divided into nights, evenings, mornings and leave. Nights are by far the busiest. We are often called out to incidents such as burglaries in progress, to respond to alarms that have gone off, or to track youths who steal cars and then abandon them and run off. The dogs are quick and efficient when searching for such people.

'At night there is also more chance for the dog to work to its full potential; there are less people around so there are less distractions for the dog when tracking and the dogs have far more scope to search and a much higher success rate. Also, with less traffic around it is obviously much easier and quicker to actually travel to the scenes of crime.

'The most rewarding parts of my job for me are when the dog succeeds in finding someone after a long search, when perhaps some of the other units will have given up. Apart from my usual police duties I also do some lecturing about my work to schools and women's groups which I also find very enjoyable.

'The saddest part of the job is when my dog dies. We build up such a close relationship with our dogs, that within 12 months of working together it's almost like we can read each other's minds. My dog lives as part of my family, travels to work with me everyday and then we work together as a team. There's such a strong bond formed it's very hard when it's broken.

'I am a Sergeant in charge of 11 other dog handlers. Further promotion for me would have meant the end of being operational with a dog, so I have chosen to stay where I am and I am very fortunate in being able to say that I have found the past 25 years extremely rewarding and that I know it was what I was meant to do'.

Note
Sergeant Lewis has written a book about his adventures with Triton, his first Police Dog. *Triton — A Police Dog's Tale* is a collection of 22 amusing stories and is available by mail order from: The Police Review Publishing Company, South Quay Plaza 2, 183 Marsh Wall, London E14 9FZ. Price £4.95 including p&p.

PRISON OFFICER DOG HANDLERS

The job

In 1967 a security report of prisons by Lord Louis Mountbatten recommended the use of dogs in HM prisons. The first dogs were multi-handled, in other words there were three handlers to one dog. In 1968 this changed to the current practice of single handling, one handler one dog.

Up until 1991 prison dogs were trained at civilian police dog schools, but since that time the prison service has had its own training school, presently situated at Melton Mowbray. In Scotland the prison dogs are trained by the RAF and Northern Ireland has its own dog school.

There are currently 430 handlers and 450 dogs working in prisons (5/94). Dogs are based at 24 prisons which regularly hold category A (high risk) prisoners.

The role of prison dogs is to act as a deterrent for both prisoners intending to escape and intruders assisting an escape. They are a mobile aid to security and a response force to alarms, incidents and escapes. The dogs normally patrol inside the prison grounds on a lead, the handlers being equipped with a radio at all times.

As well as the patrol dogs, some dogs are taught to search for drugs or firearms and explosives inside the prison. In some prisons a search programme is implemented on a regular basis, and searches could also be instigated when information has been received. Dogs can be called upon to search small areas where there is a possibility that drugs have been concealed or a whole prison can be shut down and searched from top to bottom.

All patrol dogs are trained to chase, attack and hold by the right arm. They are also trained to stand off an innocent person or a prisoner who stands still. They also search for missing property, keys, or missing persons.

German shepherds are used as patrol and search dogs and labradors and springer spaniels are trained for drugs and explosives. It is hoped that 'passive' dogs will soon be in operation on prison gates etc, having been trained specifically to indicate the presence of drugs on people, including visitors. There is a great reliance on basic obedience as the dogs must be capable of mixing with staff, inmates and visitors.

Prison dogs are either donated by the public or bought in from breeders. Ideally they would be 12-14 months old when entering the service, mature enough to stand the pressures of a basic training course. Working life expectancy is 7 years.

During the whole of its working life the dog will live at home with its handler; it is encouraged to be a working dog during the day and a family at other times. Retired dogs are very often kept by the handler as pets.

Entering the prison service

Vacancies are advertised in local press and in job centres. Applications are made directly to the local prison. Training is carried out at the Prison Service College during a 9 week residential course.

Minimum age: 20 years. No academic qualifications required.

Training to be a dog handler

Candidates for prison officer dog handlers must be established prison officers who have completed their one year probationary period. Individual prisons advertise and recruit their own staff. The applications go to a selection board and suitable candidates will be interviewed by representatives from managers of the prison and also from the dog section.

Qualities looked for
(a) a good prison officer
(b) flexibility
(c) reliability
(d) stable personality
(e) stable domestic situation (the dog will be living at home)
(f) room at home for a kennel
(g) driving licence
(h) intentions of why the applicants want to be a dog handler will be examined.

Courses

The successful applicant will commence an eight week course, with both the dog and handler being trained together. On qualification the handler receives a Home Office qualification. Drug detection dogs are 'pool' trained at the training centre and handled at non-dog prisons by ordinary members of staff. Continuation training is carried out by the Senior Officer Dog Handler back at the operational prison. After 12 to 18 months the team will return to the training school for a 2 week development course, which enhances their skills when dealing with an increased level of violence. There is one further refresher course 4-5 years after qualifying. Dog handlers often remain as such throughout their career as a prison officer. Promotion, however, is limited. There is a waiting list of serving prison officers wishing to become dog handlers.

Grades
Officer Dog Handler
   Senior Officer Dog Handler x 30 nationwide.
   Principal Officer x 3 (the country is split into 2 directorates, one Principal Officer in each plus one at the training school).
   Governor HM Prison Dogs x 1.

A day in the life of . . .
Tom Barlow, Prison Officer Dog Handler
'I have always been very interested in dogs and I was determined that if I ever got the opportunity to work with them I would take it, and now that I am I hope to stay on the dog section for the rest of my working life.

'I have been a serving Prisoner Officer for eight years and I have been a dog handler for the last three years. In order to fulfil my ambition, I applied for a vacancy that arose at another prison and I was lucky enough to get the job and worked there for some time. I moved back to my original prison when a vacancy arose.

'Like all the patrol dogs, Sarge, my second and present dog, is a German shepherd dog. I was allowed to choose him, unlike my first dog who was allocated to me. I kept Sarge at home for a few months before we started his formal training. This allowed the bond to develop and I was able to work on his nose skills and obedience. This is important because as well as being able to carry out his tasks as a working dog, he needs to be well behaved in the company of other dogs, children, sheep and horses.

'We work a shift system and my job is more or less the same day or night. It is our role to maintain security around a prison by patrolling the perimeters. We are always in contact with other Officers via a radio and there are a number of dog handlers on duty at any one time. Patrolling on your own in the middle of the night can be lonely sometimes, but you build up a close relationship with your dog who is really your working colleague. As Sarge lives at my home I am responsible for his welfare, even when I am off duty; because he needs to be fed and exercised, family life has to be adapted to fit around his needs.

'Working in all weathers can be a bit of a drag sometimes. We are however provided with wet weather clothing, but even so patrolling the perimeters of a prison can be quite cold and blowy.

'We do get to do some more light hearted things; I sometimes do talks to schools and groups about my work and we do some displays for charity events, all of which helps to raise people's awareness. We have an In-Service working trials which progresses through a series of competitions at local, regional and national level to decide the winner of the Prison Service Dogs award. The winner goes on to compete against the winners of the other services, such as the RAF and Police. Training for the event can be quite fun, and I am hoping for a lot of success with Sarge.'

DRUG DETECTION DOGS

The job

Drug detection dogs are owned and trained by the Royal Air Force at the Defence Animal Centre. They are handled and cared for on operational duties by dog handlers employed by HM Customs and Excise.

The dogs are trained to use their hunting and retrieving instincts to indicate the presence of drugs. Dogs are able to screen large areas very quickly and due to their immense olfactory system they can seek out and indicate the presence of drugs hidden in places as diverse as a car propulsion shaft and inside a human body. A drug detection dog can even indicate where someone who has drugs hidden on their person has been sitting after they have left an aeroplane, for example. The seat number would then be given to the Customs Officers who will be able to investigate further.

In 1974 two RAF dog handlers started using dogs to try to combat the rise in cannabis smuggling. By 1980 this had increased to 30 dogs nationwide and the dogs were trained to detect both cannabis and heroin. In 1981 cocaine was added to the list and during the mid to late 80s amphetamines and their derivatives were included. There are presently some 80 drug detection dogs working and this number is likely to increase in the near future.

The dogs are divided into two main categories;

- Proactive: searching planes, ships, freight, cars *etc* for drugs that might be concealed within them.

- Passive: to combat 'body packers' (people who are carrying drugs on or inside their person). The dog's indication provides a reason to search somebody.

The dogs work at airports and seaports as well as searching mail bags and anywhere else where smugglers might attempt to conceal their drugs, their handlers are in radio contact at all times so that they can react to calls for assistance from customs officers.

The drug detection dog can be thought of as a tool used to aid the customs officers in their search for illegal substances. Their job begins at the start of a search and ends at the indication of a substance or the completion of a search. When an indication is made it is logged and then handed over to the customs team working in that area.

Drug detection is very reliant on team work between the anti smuggling staff and dog teams. Every officer present at a search is responsible for the safety of the dog team, which is important when searching freight. There are two types of search: free search, which is random off-lead searching, and systematic searching, which is on the lead and therefore more controlled.

A typical day

The working day for the handlers at Felixstowe starts at 4.30am so that the teams are ready for the early morning ferries to arrive. Start times at other Customs bases or 'collections' will vary to according whether ferries, planes etc are arriving throughout the night.

The typical working day begins with an exercise period and then travel to the work area where the dog's search harness is put on. The dog is expected to search for approximately 20-25 minutes and then has a break before continuing. There will also be continuation training sessions to maintain the dog's interest and skills.

Sometimes dogs and handlers are required to go out with the display unit to shows and schools. The aim is to increase drugs awareness, to recruit new dogs and to let the public know that their help is needed to stop the trade in drugs.

Handlers are responsible for the health care and welfare of their dog, including grooming, cleaning the kennel and exercising.

Being selected as a handler

There is no direct route to becoming a drug detection dog handler. All handlers are employed by HM Customs and Excise at Administrative Officer grade and could start off their career by any one of a wide variety of jobs within Customs and Excise. As and when a dog handling vacancy becomes available it is advertised internally.

Candidates suitable for interview are selected by the personnel department. Interviews are conducted by a panel of interviewers consisting of two members of the Departmental Dog Inspectorate, the local manager and an independent person. The successful candidate is informed of the date the training course is due to start and issued with a learning pack which covers basic dog husbandry. The handler will then train at RAF Newton for approximately eight weeks with a dog that will have already been through its initial training. The last three weeks of the training consists of the new team working together under supervision in a Customs Unit.

On qualifying, all teams have to be 'passed out' by the RAF.

Job functions
Assistant Officer Drug Dog Handler.
Dog Unit Manager.

Contact
Local Customs office (can be found in your local phone book).

During a recruitment drive people are recruited for grades rather than particular posts. To help ensure success applicants should make sure they are suitable for most posts. It is possible that you could then be located in either VAT, Excise, Customs or Administration.

Qualities and qualifications
Qualification needed for AO grade
5 GCSE passes, including English.

Competencies looked for in dog handlers

- Awareness of self development.
- Oral communication skills.
- Flexibility.
- Personal organisation.
- Team worker.
- Handlers need to be agile as they are sometimes required to work in cramped conditions.

A booklet which outlines career prospects in the Customs & Excise is available from your local Customs office.

BRITISH TRANSPORT POLICE DOG HANDLERS

The job
In 1830, the Liverpool and Manchester Railway was opened by the Duke of Wellington. It was the first public railway in the world to

transport goods and passengers by locomotive, but the opening ceremony was marred by the death of the Rt. Hon. William Huskisson MP, who was killed by a passing locomotive as he alighted from the train onto the track. This accident and difficulties in crowd control on the day underlined the need for policing the railway. Within a few months the Railway Police were formed. The new force was divided into regions; in 1911 one of these, the North Eastern Railway Police, was the first police force in Britain to use dog patrols. These were Airedale Terriers and were trained to 'obey a police whistle and to chase and stop a man who is running away'.

A fascinating history of the British Transport Police is available from the Recruitment Office at the address given at the end of this section.

Today, there are some 2,200 British Transport Police. They are responsible for the safety of those travelling on the UK's rail network, including the London Underground and the European Passenger Services — 'Eurostar', through the Channel Tunnel. British Transport police dog handlers are located at all main city stations and assist policing railway property and other matters associated with the railway environment.

Patrol dogs are used in both the prevention and detection of crime. They are used for tracking suspects from the scenes of crime, chasing and stopping offenders who refuse to 'stop' when told, searching for human remains at disaster scenes and to help prevent public disorder. Specialist search dogs search for the presence of explosives.

There are currently 36 patrol dogs, all German shepherds and 22 specialist search dogs, mainly labradors and springer spaniels.

Training
Training for all patrol work takes place at the force's Dog School at Tadworth, Surrey and takes twelve weeks with a new dog. The dog and handlers also attend three weeks of refresher courses in each year and continuation training each month. Explosive training is carried out at a designated Home Office explosives training centre. After completing their training, the dog and handler will be licensed by the Home Office. The dogs live at home with their handlers, who each have a marked police van.

Entering the Transport Police Force
Applicants make a written request to the Recruitment Office for an application form. They will then receive either a letter stating appli-

cations are not being processed at present or a 22 page application form. On returning the form (providing the applicant meets the selection criteria) they are called to sit the Common Police Entrance Exam. On completion there will then be an interview and the applicants will be vetted. If successful at this stage they will then be invited to a 2 day selection assessment at Tadworth, the force's training centre, to see if they possess the character traits and skills and physical fitness required of a police officer.

Having passed this assessment the applicant will have a final interview and a full medical — they will then be offered an appointment. About 2% of all those who apply to the recruitment office in the first instance reach this stage.

On entering the Transport Police, the candidate goes through a two year probationary period. Basic training is based on seven modules over 32 weeks in accordance with Home Office policy. The modules include a ten week and five week period at a Home Office District Police Training Centre. On completion of the module training three two week post foundation courses occur within the two year probation period. Selection into specialised areas, such as dog handling, would not take place until after the two year probationary period, and usually not until at least five years after qualification. Competition for a specialist post is keen, but all posts are filled on ability and merit.

Qualities required

- No criminal record (including some motoring offences).

- There is no height restriction.

- Minimum age is 18 years, 6 months; the maximum age limit is 45 years.

- There is officially no sex/race discrimination within the Force.

Applicants must be sociable, confident, caring, and demonstrate a flexible approach to people, but must also be capable of dealing with very stressful situations such as bomb scares and suicides.

Becoming a dog handler

Posts are advertised in the Transport Police internal *Force Orders*. Applicants are interviewed at the Dog School and their ability as a police officer will be examined. This aspect is more important than previous experience with dogs. Remember it can take many years before a police officer is successful in becoming a dog handler.

An information booklet, *British Transport Police: A Force On The Move*, and further details can be obtained from: Force Recruitment Officer, British Transport Police Headquarters, PO Box 260, 15 Tavistock Place, London WC1H 9SJ.

A day in the life of . . .

PC Judy Bailey, British Transport Police, Specialist Search Dog Handler

'My job as a specialist search dog handler is, with the aid of my dog, to find bombs and explosives that have been planted either on or around railway property. My dog searches an area and indicates the position of a bomb. The bomb disposal officers are informed and they deal with making it safe. In contrast to uniformed patrol dog handlers, whose function is to deter, we keep a very low profile.

'I have been in the Force for thirteen years: two years in uniform during my probationary period, eight years in CID and three years on the dog section. Although I had originally wanted to be a dog handler, I was channelled into CID. However, now I'm here I wouldn't want to do anything else.

'My first dog was a German shepherd patrol dog. I thoroughly enjoyed my time as a patrol dog handler. It's very different to what I do now. It's very much in the front line; you are dealing with the general public all of the time and so I think people skills, as well as dog handling skills, are very important. You have to be proven as a patrol dog handler before being considered as a specialist dog handler.

'My training as a specialist dog handler was carried out at Stafford, at a Home Office training school, over an eight week period. As well as the dog training we also had to learn about different explosives and their accompanying devices. I was matched with seven other dogs before George, my present dog; the others were all in someway unsuitable for the job. The dogs we use need to demonstrate an incredibly strong drive to search — they must want to get what they are looking for so much they would go through a brick wall to get it. George, an English springer spaniel, was donated by a couple from Gloucestershire who found he was too boisterous for them. When I was in training I kept in touch with them to let them know how he progressed.

'The dogs are put under a lot of pressure during the training period. Stamina is important, as is the dog's age — it must not be too immature otherwise it would have very short concentration spans and general control would be lacking. Conversely it cannot be too old, otherwise it's potential working life is reduced.

'We work in pairs for safety and to ensure that the searches are carried out systematically. My partner is Steve. He has a collie called Sheppie who started life as a stray. One handler acts as a 'spotter' for the other, pointing out possible search areas whilst being alert to possible safety hazards. After a period, the roles are reversed and the second handler will work their dog whilst the first dog is rested to prevent nasal fatigue. My day varies enormously, depending on a number of things including VIP movements, security alerts and bomb threats.

'There are a number of dedicated specialist dog handlers based in the south of England and we have a reciprocal arrangement with the civilian police if extra numbers are needed. We sometimes have to fill in for our colleagues in other parts of the country, so as you might expect we do an enormous amount of travelling, approximately 1,500 miles per week.

'The most satisfying and challenging part of my job is actually carrying out a search for a bomb. I admit you probably have to be a bit mad to go in when everyone else is trying to get out as fast as possible! We wear bomb-proof suits when searching, but really your life is in your dog's hands. You have to have absolute trust in them. To do the job the handlers have to be extremely placid, calm, methodical and able to work under extreme pressure.

'One of the most stressful parts of the job is our annual test — we are licensed by the Home Office and that licence is renewed every year. If you fail the test, you will be transferred from the dog section for good. We are tested regularly to make sure that the best possible standards are being met. The whole experience is far more frightening than searching for a live bomb!

'The dogs live at home with their handlers and go everywhere with them. They become very much part of family life. When working they must be very responsive to commands so as to prevent them from being injured; there are often dangers such as live railway tracks to be avoided. The dog always works within our sight which not only helps to ensure their safety but allows us to recognise their signal when they find a device. George loves searching, it is pure pleasure for him. He will ignore anything like food that he comes across in the process of a search. We train them by building up an obsession with a toy which is then associated with the presence of explosives until the explosives themselves will trigger the desired response. On finding the explosives, the toy then appears via the handler as a reward.

'We generally work a shift pattern, although we are on 24 hour call, and frequently have to work weekends and evenings. Obviously we have to be reactive to whatever is going on at that time.'

THE DEFENCE ANIMAL CENTRE

The Defence Animal Centre is a joint operation between the Army and the Royal Air Force and is based at the Defence Animal Centre, Melton Mowbray (Leicestershire) with a satellite dog training wing at RAF Newton (Nottinghamshire). The Defence Animal Centre is responsible for training all the dogs for the armed services, including Ministry of Defence Guard Service, Customs & Excise, Ministry of Defence Police as well as other agencies at home and abroad.

The RAF and the Army have over 2,000 trained dogs working worldwide between them.

The details that follow for each of the services are correct at the time of going to press but as the Defence Animal Centre is in the process of rationalisation details may well be subject to change. For the latest details please consult your local Careers Information Office.

Dogs are donated to the Defence Animal Centre by the general public. Of the 1,000 dogs that are donated annually (aged between 12 months and three years) around 450 are suitable for training. On arrival dogs spend three weeks in quarantine, during which time they will be assessed; if they are selected they will be trained for specific duties, which could be:

- basic protection
- arms & explosives detection
- drug detection
- police dogs for Ministry of Defence and Military Police use (search/track/protection)
- vehicle search
- tracking
- immigrant detection
- passive search.

ROYAL ARMY VETERINARY CORPS

The job
The RAVC is dedicated to the employment of animals in the armed services and is one of the smallest Corps in the British Army.

Applying for assessment

The first step to a career in the RAVC is to express a desire at your nearest high street Army Recruitment Office. After an initial assessment at the office, which includes a computer touch test, a medical screen and an informal interview, a 24 hour selection takes place at one of the four recruit selection centres. Here, a full medical is carried out as well as physical tests and an interview by a Personnel Selection Officer. Following this there is a ten week military training course at a base training camp, after which you would move on to the Defence Animal Centre.

Basic training

The basic grade at this point is ATA (Animal Technical Assistant). ATAs care for and maintain service animals (dogs and/or horses). The training consists of a two week dog handling course, a veterinary and equine course and kennel management. ATAs are then taught to be assistant trainers (*ie* acting as the 'criminal' in a padded suit) and then how to train a protection dog.

ATAs and dog trainers are employed in the UK, Germany, Cyprus and Hong Kong. At this point they are called ATA Class 3 trained RAVC Soldiers.

After this first stage all ATAs spend a further six months training protection dogs under supervision. At the end of that six months, the soldiers will be directed into one or two ways:

1. Those who have shown an ability to be dog trainers spend six months producing protection dogs and a further six months training specialist dogs under supervision. After successful completion of this stage they then do a written, oral and practical examination, on successful completion of which they become Class 2 Dog Trainers. The following two years are spent producing specialist and other dogs within the services, qualifying as an instructor and gaining a knowledge of all matters relating to dogs within the services. On completion of two years successful on-job assessment, they sit a further examination to become Class 1 Dog Trainers.

2. The remaining ATAs complete a six month period of training protection dogs under supervision. They then spend twelve months assisting dog trainers in the production of trained dogs and also study advanced animal care and kennel management. They then take the Class 2 examination.

On passing this examination they also help in the training of the specialist dogs. After two years on job assessment they help in the training of specialist dogs and can sit the ATA Class 1 examination. During this period there is an opportunity to undertake a specialist dog training course leading to qualification as an operational specialist dog handler.

Both ATAs and dog trainers are on the same level of pay until a dog trainer becomes a full corporal (after Class 1), when they then go up to a higher pay band.

Promotion grades

Private to Warrant Officer Class 1, where there is a small chance of gaining a Commission.

Promotion within the Army often means moving away from dog related posts into man-management.

Qualifications include Regimental, Trade and Educational proficiency.

Qualities required

- a genuine concern for animals
- passion for the job
- motivation
- some experience to prove that you can relate to animals
- a hard worker
- a team worker
- maturity
- a love of outdoor life.

Physical qualities

Min height: 152 cm
Min weight: 50kg
Min age: 17.5 years
Max age: 25 years

There is no sex restriction and the applicant must be British.

Other opportunities within the Army

Royal Military Police Dog Handlers, part of the Adjutant General's Corps. RMP use dogs for drugs and explosives searches.

Pioneer Corps, part of the Royal Logistics Corps — secure military establishments.

Details of both from your local Army Careers Office.

ROYAL AIR FORCE POLICE DOG HANDLER

The job
Situations available:

- RAF Police Dog Handler
- Kennel Staff

The Defence Animal Section Newton Wing is located at RAF Newton, Nottinghamshire. Here Royal Air Force Police dog handlers and their dogs are trained together.

There are no formal qualifications necessary for selection to the trades of Royal Air Force Police (RAFP) and kennel assistant. However, you are required to pass a short series of tests at a Careers Information Office. Minimum height regulations exist for the RAFP trades and you need to have normal colour vision. Minor visual defects (distant vision) which can be corrected by the wearing of spectacles or contact lenses may be acceptable.

After selection and successful completion of six weeks recruit training, you receive your basic trade training at the RAFP school.

Basic RAFP Trade Training Course
This course lasts eight and a half weeks and provides the professional knowledge and skills necessary for coping with all the situations likely to be encountered in the early years of RAFP service. Training will include instruction and practice in the use of weapons for both airmen and airwomen.

All RAFP must be qualified to drive light vehicles. Therefore, you must hold either a current full or provisional driving licence, normally free from endorsements.

Dog handling
On completion of basic trade training those airmen/airwomen in the RAFP trade who have volunteered for dog handling duties will be required to complete a further seven week course of training, and teaming with a RAFP dog.

Patrol dogs
During the early part of the Second World War (1939-45), the potential was recognised for using properly trained teams of police dogs and handlers for safeguarding airfield installations and equipment against sabotage and theft, and at the same time achieving a

significant economy in manpower. Subsequently the Ministry of Aircraft Production Guard Dog School was formed in November 1941 to train police dog handler teams for employment at Royal Air Force installations throughout the world. In 1946 the responsibility for training was transferred to the Royal Air Force Police and remained so until April 1991 when the Defence Animal Centre was formed.

Search dogs
Corporals selected for specialisation in this field go through a very rigorous and thorough twelve week course.

During the drug course they train their dogs, under expert supervision, to detect cannabis, heroin, cocaine and amphetamines. Those on the FX course train their dogs to detect firearms and explosives.

On successful completion of the basic trade training course you will graduate as a leading aircraftman/leading aircraftwoman. However, airmen and airwomen in the RAFP trade are appointed to the rank of acting corporal (unpaid). To qualify for promotion to the next rank of senior aircraftman/senior aircraftwomen you will be required to pass a trade ability test, which is an examination based on the duties of your trade and is held at RAF units. Once you have passed this examination promotion can take place after a minimum of 12 months' total service.

Further promotion is by selection in competition with others after passing the appropriate education tests, and subject to successful completion of a further training course (RAFP trade only), general service training courses (all trades), and a trade management training course (RAFP trades only). There are opportunities for promotion to the rank of warrant officer for both airmen and airwomen in the RAFP trade.

Kennel assistants

Most kennel assistants are employed at the Dog Training Wing of the Defence Animal Centre where they exercise, groom, feed and attend to RAF Police dogs awaiting handlers. Each kennel assistant is responsible for a number of dogs and their kennel accommodation. They must possess basic veterinary knowledge to enable them to recognise signs and symptoms of illness in the dogs, and to maintain good standards of hygiene. There are opportunities for kennel assistants to serve abroad. Usual working hours are 8am to 5pm Monday to Friday, with one weekend duty in every four. Kennel assistants have quarters on the base.

Basic kennel assistant trade training course

This course lasts three weeks at the RAFP School and includes the handling, grooming, exercising and feeding of RAFP dogs and basic veterinary instruction to enable you to recognise the symptoms of illness.

There are limited opportunities for promotion to the rank of sergeant in the kennel assistant trade. In addition, after a minimum of two years' service some kennel assistants are permitted to apply for selection to RAFP in the rank of SAC/SACW.

Much of the above information is taken from the RAF Careers leaflet no. 359, available from RAF Careers Offices.

A day in the life of . . .

Flight Sergeant Ken Dowers, Patrol Supervisor
'I'm not really able to describe a typical day as patrol dogs only work at night! We work between 6pm and 8am in six hour shifts and sleep during the day.

'One hour before going on duty, handlers arrive and are armed, briefed and then prepare their dog, which is kept kennelled at the base. Four dog teams work six-hour stints with two half-hour breaks. The work can be tedious; the handlers are trained for the unexpected but the unexpected actually rarely happens, not surprisingly as the whole purpose of the RAF police dog is for it to be a deterrent. We work four nights, three evenings and then four days off.

'The dogs "catnap" during the day — bearing in mind that they are working during the night and alert during the day to the comings and goings of other staff. During their stand down periods, the handlers groom, do continuation training and generally check all is well with their dogs. To ensure that the dogs are maintained at the required standard we do three hours of continuation training every three weeks and are regularly tested by the Provost Marshall Dog Inspectorate.'

4
Working for Assistance Organisations

In this chapter we will look at the main career opportunities for working with dogs in the various assistance organisations. In particular we will discuss:

- working with guide dogs for the blind
- working with dogs for the disabled
- working with support dogs
- working with hearing dogs for the deaf

ASSISTANCE DOGS (UK)

Assistance Dogs (UK) was launched on 23rd April 1994 and incorporates The Guide Dogs for the Blind Association, Hearing Dogs for the Deaf, Dogs for the Disabled and Support Dogs, all of which are registered and established charities. The purpose of Assistance Dogs (UK) is to enhance the quality of life of the people who rely on the dogs specially trained by the charities by helping them to achieve greater independence.

THE GUIDE DOGS FOR THE BLIND ASSOCIATION

The guide dogs story began in Britain with a meeting in 1930 between three women: Miss Muriel Cooke and Mrs Rosamund Bond, both dog enthusiasts, and Mrs Dorothy Eustis. Mrs Eustis was a Swiss lady who, having seen guide dogs being trained in Germany, had trained some herself in the USA. Mrs Eustis offered the services of a trainer, and the first class of four owners and their dogs completed their training in July 1931. The school was based at a lock up garage in Wallasey. After the outbreak of the Second World War in 1939 the operation moved to Leamington Spa and since then an additional six regional training centres and six smaller centres have opened, and there are plans for more to follow.

During the 1960s a puppy-walking and breeding scheme was developed and GDBA opened its own Breeding Centre at Tollgate House, near Warwick in 1969, breeding some 1,000 puppies every year, around 75% of which will qualify as guide dogs.

The job
The aim of Guide Dogs for the Blind is to promote and provide independent mobility to visually impaired people through guide dog ownership.

This involves;

- breeding & selecting suitable dogs

- training those dogs to act as guides for visually impaired people

- matching them to their future owners' needs

- training dogs and their owners to work safely and effectively together, and

- supporting qualified guide dogs and their owners in their home environment.

Training
Each regional training centre has around ten periods each year where classes of visually impaired students attend up to four weeks of residential training, in which all staff are involved.

The main activities of the staff are;

- training and supporting visually impaired clients
- fund raising, public relations and administration
- breeding, training and care of dogs.

The seven main training centres are in Forfar, Middlesborough, Leamington Spa, Wokingham, Exeter, Bolton and NE London (Redbridge), and the Breeding Centre near Leamington Spa. There are small centres based in Nottingham, Cardiff, Belfast, Maidstone, Southampton, Larkhall (in Strathclyde) and Liverpool.

Job functions

Kennel staff

Kennel staff, who are required to 'live in' at one of the centres, start work at 7am. Most are in charge of allocated kennel blocks and are responsible for the cleaning out, grooming and feeding of the dogs in their care.

Kennel staff work alternate weekends. As the visually impaired students are resident at the centre during their training, kennel staff are expected to help out at meal times.

Internal courses provide theoretical and practical training to prepare staff for the City & Guilds/NCVQ qualification. There are promotional opportunities in kennel management with two kennel supervisors, an assistant kennel manager and a kennel manager at each centre. Training as a veterinary nurse is available externally.

- *Skills required*: domestic or other experience with dogs. Good health and fitness. GCSE English and Maths or the equivalent. Minimum age 18 yrs.

- *Qualities required*: team worker, practical, caring towards both dogs and people. Independent enough to live away from home.

Guide dog trainer

Guide dog trainers are responsible for introducing young adult dogs to basic guiding skills. These include obstacle avoidance, traffic awareness, building concentration and confidence. The dogs trained by the trainers are assessed before they are handed on to instructors who carry out the advanced training and matching to the eventual guide dog owner.

Guide dog trainers are trained to City & Guilds/NCVQ standard.

Promotion to senior guide dog trainer is the most obvious career progression although it is possible for guide dog trainers to go on to become apprentice guide dog mobility instructors. Promotion is also possible to the position of puppy walking supervisor, responsible for the puppies currently being socialised by the volunteer puppy walkers.

Qualifications

GCSE standard education including Maths and English, and preferably a science subject, or equivalent. Full driving licence. Minimum age 18 yrs.

Qualities required
Must be articulate and confident, literate and numerate; in good health and have stamina. Must enjoy working out of doors in all weathers; must be an experienced handler and enjoy working alone.

Guide dog mobility instructors
Guide dog mobility instructors train visually impaired people to achieve independence through the use of guide dogs. Guide dog mobility instructors have intensive spells of training both dogs and visually impaired people. They will also visit established guide dog owners at home. There is a 37 month apprenticeship covering dog care skills, dog training and teaching visually impaired people how to use a dog.

Prospects for further development into one of the following areas are good:

● *Dog supply supervisor*
Responsible for the trainers on the dog supply unit.

● *Area supervisor*
Responsible for a small team of GDMIs and the guide dog owners within their own allocated geographical area.

● *Regional training manager*
Responsible for the training and care of dogs and the guide dog owners within their region.

Qualifications required
5 GCSEs including English & Maths and supported by a science subject and ideally a social science. Minimum age 18 years. Full driving licence.

Qualities required
Strong interpersonal skills and excellent communication skills. Must be sympathetic to the objectives of the Association; be experienced/adaptable in dealing with animals and people. Be able to work hard and work alone but as a member of a team.

Other information
There are also job functions such as; accountancy, fund raising, public relations, secretarial, personnel, data processing, and estates management.

This information is based on the careers pamphlet available from: The Guide Dogs for the Blind Association, Hillfields, Burghfield, Reading, Berks. Tel: (01734) 835555.

A day in the life of . . .

Janis Battersby, Centre Manager, Nottingham GDBA Training Centre

'I am living proof that there are promotion opportunities within the GDBA! I began working for the Association twenty years ago as a part-time domestic at the Leamington Spa training centre. I became fascinated with the training that I saw going on around me and applied to become a Training Assistant on what was then called the "Early Training Unit" (nowadays called the Dog Supply Unit).

'I spent four happy years as a trainer and then applied for an apprenticeship to become a mobility instructor. After qualification, I went on to be an area supervisor, staff training officer, dog supply supervisor and then centre manager here at Nottingham.

'The small centres, like Nottingham, work on the same principle as the regional centres, carrying out the same activities only on a smaller scale. Because we train fewer people on our classes, we are better able to tailor the training to meet the needs of the individual, particularly those who may need more personal attention because of added disabilities. The small centres were opened to act as a support to their regional centres and to ensure that we continue to provide a personal service as the Association grows.

'Our dogs are supplied by our parent centre at Leamington Spa and come to us when they have completed their early training. As with regional centres, we have ten classes per year, but with a maximum of four people on each class who train at the centre for the first twelve days and then continue their training at home.

'The staff here are very team/family orientated and work closely together, filling in for each other when absences occur. All technical staff do a weekend duty on a rota system, but the usual working week is from Monday to Friday. It is very important for small centre staff to be extremely flexible and adaptable, and essential that they are team players and are prepared to muck in and do whatever is necessary.

'My own job is very reactive. It is very difficult to maintain a daily routine as we are here to provide a service and if a problem arises, whether with a guide dog owner or a dog in training, they must take priority over everything else.

'The best part of my job is the variety. I head all the departments

— training, fund raising and domestic — and enjoy the close contact that I have with my staff and the guide dog owners in our region.'

DOGS FOR THE DISABLED

The job

Dogs for the Disabled is a registered charity formed in 1986 by Francis Hay, a dog lover who was disabled with bone marrow cancer. The aim of Dogs for the Disabled is to train specially selected dogs to perform tasks which persons with disabilities find difficult or impossible to do for themselves and to provide those people with companionship, independence and security. The dogs are trained to:

● retrieve cordless phones

● open and close doors

● retrieve letters and newspapers from letter boxes and to pick up accidentally dropped articles

● activate light switches

● with the aid of a special harness, help a person with a balance problem walk without the aid of a walking frame or stick.

Since July 1994, Dogs for the Disabled has contracted Guide Dogs for the Blind Association to train all of its dogs and clients, retaining its own staff, office and fund-raisers.

There are currently two training centres, one in Exeter and one at Leamington Spa, which is also the organisation's head office.

Dogs for the Disabled has seven fund raising branches around the country which raise money to fund the charity.

The number of dogs trained annually is rising steadily; there were sixteen in 1993 and eighteen in 1994. There are currently over sixty Dogs for the Disabled working in the UK.

Puppies selected for training are puppy walked in private homes for the first year of their lives before coming into the centre for training. They start with four months of basic training, learning how to hold, how to pull, traffic socialisation, how to walk with wheel-chairs, how to walk on the right and other skills. The dogs are then matched with a potential client prior to their advanced training. For two months the dog will be specifically trained to suit that person's particular requirements.

Job functions

- fund raising
- clerical
- trainers (part time & full time) (2)
- instructors (3)
- senior instructor (1)
- training manager.

Experience required

Trainers — experience with dogs in some form, preferably in a training field.

Instructors — a combination of dog training experience and people skills. Empathy with disabled people is essential. A team worker and a communicator who is prepared to ask questions.

Age preferred

Mid 20s to late 30s.

Qualifications required

5 GCSEs, preferably including English and Maths. Driving licence.

Training given

2.5 year apprenticeship to be an instructor. This is in three stages: (1) very basic obedience and kennel experience, (2) basic training, (3) client training.

The stages are not exam based, although written tests do occur and there is an exam at the end of the apprenticeship. You can be asked to leave if tests are failed.

Jobs advertised

Locally, then in the dog orientated publications.

Further information

Send enquiries to: Linda Hams (Training Manager), Dogs for the Disabled, Frances Hay House, Bishops Tachbrook, Leamington Spa, Warwickshire CV33 9UQ. Tel: (01926) 651179.

A newsletter is available from Dogs for the Disabled on receipt of a stamped addressed envelope (7x10").

A day in the life of . . .

Helen McCain, Senior Instructor, Dogs for the Disabled

'I am actually employed by Guide Dogs for the Blind. I qualified at the Exeter Centre as a guide dog trainer and I am now on a permanent secondment to Dogs for the Disabled. After qualifying I then decided that I wanted another challenge, but wasn't sure if I wanted an apprenticeship to be a guide dog mobility instructor. When the opportunity of the secondment came up I applied for it!

'I am the senior instructor, which entails selecting the dogs and being in charge of both their training and that of the apprentice trainers. I also interview the prospective disabled clients and carry out their eventual training with a fully trained dog. Of course there is all the paperwork that goes with all these things. Sometimes I feel as if I am being pulled in many different directions, but having said that, I find it extremely fulfilling. The idea of dogs aiding people as Dogs for the Disabled is a relatively new concept and I really feel I am achieving something in areas that have not been tackled before.

'My job is very reactive to whatever is happening at the time, although I do try to keep to a routine when I have dogs to train. I moved into the Leamington Spa area specifically for the job, which has become my life, I suppose. When I need a break from it I usually go right away from the area otherwise I tend to think about work and plan things even when I'm not supposed to be working.

'There is a strong team spirit at the centre. It's essential that everyone pulls together and communication is important so as to make sure we're all pulling in the same direction.

'Although we have a separate fund raising department I still sometimes give talks to interested bodies and I man the publicity stand at Guide Dog Open Days, Crufts and so on. From time to time I am required to do radio and television interviews, which are great for raising people's awareness of Dogs for the Disabled.'

SUPPORT DOGS

Support Dogs is based in South Yorkshire and covers the North East and Midlands areas of the United Kingdom. It provides training for disabled people and their own dogs. There is currently one main training centre, with training being co-ordinated from other sites in the region. More sites are planned.

In the first two years of Support Dogs being in operation there are already some 20 dogs working and at various stages of training; this will increase substantially in the coming few years.

Many disabled people already have a dog which is an extremely valuable companion and with whom they have a very special bond. This bond is utilised by Support Dogs by channelling the dog's willingness to help into true assistance work.

Other advantages of training the disabled person with their own dog are:

- As the dog is already living with the disabled person he will have adapted to their limitations and way of life.

- The dog will be trained in a familiar environment and with the person he will always be working with.

- As the disabled person is involved in the training he understands how the dog learns and is therefore able to reinforce the training wherever necessary.

Support dogs also help disabled people who do not own a dog but would like to be considered for the scheme to find a compatible companion, be it a puppy or older dog.

Training

The training takes about twelve months and costs around £500; all the funding is by donations, the organisation being a registered charity.

Having assessed each individual dog and owner a Support Dog can be trained to:

- pick up dropped objects
- fetch named articles (hair brush, cordless telephone, *etc*)
- fetch the phone when it rings
- switch lights on and off
- raise the alarm if the owner falls out of a chair
- act as a support
- press lift buttons
- go into shops such as the Post Office for stamps or pension
- open and close doors
- do any other tasks which may help the owner

The correct relationship between dog and owner is achieved through the normal routes of feeding, games and attention, grooming, and sleeping areas. Socialisation plays a very important part of the training. These dogs will accompany their owners to public places and so have to be reliable in all kinds of situations. At every training session a new socialisation exercise is undertaken but specific field trips are also undertaken, for example to shopping malls, cafes or restaurants. The dogs are also made familiar with a variety of other animals.

Job functions

- clerical
- fund raising
- apprentice trainers
- trainers.

Still in its formative years, Support Dogs currently employs three apprentices and a training manager. Staff requirements will grow along with the increase in training centres.

Jobs are first advertised in the local press and then in the dog press.

Qualities looked for

Most importantly, people skills. Dog handling skills can be taught but people skills must already be apparent. It is important that any applicant is willing to learn about, and be interested in, disabilities. Trainers will be working on a one to one basis with the disabled client and must be able to deal with whatever disability may be present. Family problems may arise as the client is going through his/her training and the trainer must be able to deal with such situations. The applicant must also be a good team worker and dedicated to the cause.

Qualifications required

No formal qualifications are required but applicants must hold a current driving licence, be capable of writing clear and readable reports, and able to read a map. They must also be on the telephone at home.

A first aid certificate is not a necessity but it will help.

Training available

There is a structured 21 month apprenticeship, conducted under the guidance of the training manager.

Stage 1 — The first 3 months are a probationary period

Stage 2 — The following 6 months follow on from stage 1, as a Trainee Support Dog Trainer.

Stage 3 — The trainee is then working with disabled people as their dogs for 1 year under the direct supervision of the Training Manager. There is an oral test, assessed by the Training Manager and a disabled person, based on knowledge of disabilities.

Further details

Enquiries should be made to: Support Dogs, PO Box 447, Sheffield S7 2YY. Tel: (0114) 2320026.

HEARING DOGS FOR THE DEAF

In 1979 Professor Lee Bustead, Dean of the School of Veterinary Medicine at Washington State University spoke at the British Small Animal Veterinary Association International Symposium. The paper included reference to training schemes in the United States in which dogs were trained to assist deaf people. Bruce Fogle, a veterinary surgeon, heard the paper and on his return contacted Lady Wright of the Royal National Institute for the Deaf.

Consequently, Hearing Dogs for the Deaf was officially launched in 1982 following visits by Bruce Fogle and Lady Wright to hearing dogs training centres in the United States. With help and advice from the American Hearing Ears Scheme, the first centre was set up in Oxfordshire.

Since 1 in 8 people in Britain suffer from a significant hearing loss there is a huge number of potential recipients for hearing dogs. There are currently some 250 hearing dogs working and 70 dogs are trained annually.

Hearing dogs are mostly unwanted dogs obtained from rescue centres. They are often cross breeds and are usually small or medium in size. The dog must be sound of temperament and naturally inquisitive. Guarding breeds are not used as they have the potential to be overprotective and tend to react very quickly to stimuli. Some deaf people are quite nervous and too much reaction could then cause problems.

Hearing dogs are well trained to alert the recipients to everyday sounds, such as:

- alarm clock
- doorbell

- telephone
- smoke alarm
- baby alarm
- cooker timer

On hearing a specific sound, the dogs are taught to communicate with their owners by touch and then to lead them to the sound source.

Having been obtained by the organisation, dogs are socialised for as long as necessary in a puppy socialiser's home in order to assess the temperament. If the dog is the right age, it will go on to 16 weeks' training at the training centre, the first two weeks of which comprise the trainer's assessment of the dog's suitability for training. During this time it will wear a 'hearing dogs in training' lead slip. Only after the final assessment in the recipient's home (three months after completing training) will it wear the instantly recognisable hearing dogs coat.

There are currently two training centres: Lewknor in Oxfordshire (which is also the Head Office) and Cliffe in North Yorkshire, opened in 1994.

Job functions

Puppy socialisers

There are currently some 40 puppy socialisers, increasing to 100 by the end of 1994 to meet the additional demands of the new training centre. All puppy socialisers are voluntary but do have the dogs food supplied and receive assistance towards other costs. All live within 25 miles of Lewknor and are visited monthly by the puppy socialising officer. They also attend monthly puppy classes at Lewknor.

The puppy socialisers may have a dog from anything between one and eight months. It is their job to ensure that the dog is well socialised, behaves acceptably in public places, and can settle happily into a domestic environment. It is usual for the recipient to remain in contact with their dog's puppy socialisers.

A *puppy socialising officer* is responsible for all the puppy socialisers.

Fund raising

There are fund raising branches all over the country which work hard to raise the £2,500 it takes to train each dog. The branches are run by volunteers and are co-ordinated from the Centre at Lewknor. A leaflet is available from Hearing Dogs about how you could help.

Kennel staff
This consists of one kennel supervisor and one member of staff. A driving licence is required.

Hearing dog trainers
They are responsible for the training of the dogs and are also responsible for the recipients during the recipient's five day stay at the training centre. The trainer has a six month training programme following three months of probation and an appraisal. During their training period, trainers are supervised by experienced staff. All training staff are required to learn sign language. It is possible to progress on to the position of senior trainer or placement officer.

Placement officers
Placement officers are responsible for making support training visits to the recipient's home during the first month — this involves travelling and staying away from home for a few days at a time. They also carry out annual visits to recipients.

Training supervisor
This person oversees the puppy socialisation scheme and training of all dogs and recipients, liaising with different departments, checking records and so on.

Training manager
Oversees everything from choosing puppies to retiring old dogs.

Skills required

- Dog experience and/or experience with disabled people.

- Applicants must be adaptable and be able to work as part of a team.

- Good communication skills including particularly clear speech are essential.

- A driving licence is essential.

  Minimum age: 18 years
  Vacancies advertised: Local press, dog magazines and papers.

Additional job functions
Accounting, Clerical, Deaf Liaison (carries out initial interviews with prospective recipients), Administration.

Further information
Enquiries should be made to: Training Manager, Hearing Dogs for the Deaf, London Road, Lewknor, Oxon. Tel: (01844) 353898.

A newsletter is available — write to the address above to be put on the mailing list.

A day in the life of . . .
Wendy Stratford, Senior Trainer, Hearing Dogs for the Deaf
'I came to Hearing Dogs about three years ago, having previously worked in boarding kennels for seven years. It was whilst I was doing a small animal care course that I did a project on hearing dogs and became interested from then on.

'My training was very good; I was well supported and received lots of feed back and help from other staff — there is a real team spirit within the organisation.

'I work from 9am to 5pm Monday to Friday, and we have a rota for weekend kennel duties, which is one in four weekends. I also do some evening work when we do talks to groups such as Lions Clubs, WIs etc.

'Like the other trainers, I have four dogs at any one time who are all at different stages of training. We aim to give them two training sessions each day and an obedience session. We have to take the dogs to any places where the prospective recipient may take it, *eg* on buses and in shops, to make sure that the dog is well behaved in those areas. We often work in pairs so that, for example, someone else can be ringing the doorbell whilst I am handling/training/rewarding the dog and vice versa.

'After two weeks of assessment and training, the dog will be matched to a potential recipient. The recipient will then be invited into the centre for half a day to meet and walk the dog and chat about the type of place they live in and the exact sounds that the dog would need to respond to, reaffirming all the recipient's initial interview details. We are then able to train the dog to work to their specific needs. At the end of the dog's training period, the recipient will be invited to come to train at the centre for five days and the training is then continued in their home by a placement officer.

'The best bits of my job are working with different dogs and working out what is going to motivate each one the best. It is very satisfying to see a dog with a recipient, knowing it is going to change their life for the better.

'If I *had* to find a negative point, it would be finding the time to get everything done, making sure your dogs get out enough and all the necessary paper work is kept up to date.'

5
Working for Welfare Organisations

Many satisfying careers can be enjoyed working with one or other of the animal welfare organisations. In this chapter we will discuss the work, and employment opportunities, within the best known ones:

● The Royal Society for the Prevention of Cruelty to Animals (RSPCA)

● The National Canine Defence League (NCDL)

● Blue Cross

● Wood Green Animal Shelters

● The Dogs' Home, Battersea

THE ROYAL SOCIETY FOR THE PREVENTION OF CRUELTY TO ANIMALS

The RSPCA is the world's largest animal welfare organisation. It was founded in 1824 to promote kindness and prevent cruelty to animals. There are 207 RSPCA branches throughout England and Wales, each branch being a charity in its own right. All branches make an annual donation to the national Society and run their own animal homes, clinic or welfare/advice centres. There are several sections of the RSPCA, dealing with domestic pets, farm animals, wildlife, research animals, education, legislation and international support.

All the branches fall within regions and these in turn look to the head office at Horsham in Sussex for the overall management of the Society. The head office is responsible for all major decisions and big campaigns.

There are 54 animal homes throughout England and Wales where animals are cared for until, hopefully, homes can be found for them. Prospective owners are given a home-check before they are allowed to adopt an animal and it is subsequently visited once settled in its new home.

Each branch has a committee which is run according to RSPCA policy. The committee is made up of volunteers, all of whom are able to give constructive input into the running of the branch. Many have expertise in the commercial world which can be put to good use.

The following staff details are based on the Leicester Branch of the RSPCA. All branches will differ to some degree, but this should give a good basic illustration of the kind of organisation involved.

Job functions

Branch manager — appointed by the committee
Assistant to the branch manager (part time)
Administration staff (2)
Kennel manageress
Assistant kennel manageress
Cattery manageress
Kennel/cattery assistants
Voluntary helpers.

Voluntary opportunities

Kennel help (over 14 years)
Work experience from schools
Fund raising
Home visitors.
Volunteers are assessed by the Branch Manager to see where they could be best suited.

Kennel staff

Qualities looked for: common sense and intelligence. Experience with dogs is useful; you would need to be realistic about the working conditions and be a team worker. A driving licence is preferred. You should also have a cheerful disposition, be able to read/write English, and be a good communicator (able to deal with the public as well as other staff).

Training

Staff are given a six month structured training programme. The first three months are probationary, and then a further three months under supervision taking animals right through to the point of sale.

- Vacancies advertised: local press
- Managerial positions: national press

Further Information

There is an RSPCA Animal Action Club for young people up to 17 years to age. Contact your local branch for details.

Head Office: RSPCA, Causeway, Horsham, West Sussex RH12 1HG. Tel: (01403) 64181.

A day in the life of . . .

Kirstyn Markillie, Kennel Assistant, RSPCA Leicester

'I first came here seven years ago on leaving school — I had been to work here previously on a work experience placement and knew it was what I wanted to do. I came from a very dog loving family — we had four Newfoundlands, one Beagle X, one Whippet X, five cats and a rabbit! I had been telling everyone since junior school that I would work with animals. Unfortunately my senior school was not very helpful but luckily my parents were very supportive.

'We all have our own block (I am in charge of the puppy block) but we are all trained to work in each and the cattery so that we are interchangeable if someone is sick or on holiday. I have a flat here at the kennels which means that if we have a sick dog in kennels I am able to check on it during the night.

'We start the day at 9am. The pups all have their breakfast and are let out. Their kennels are then cleaned and the water bowls are re-filled. The puppies are then let back in and the outside runs cleaned. All through the day I am also dealing with people coming in to look at the pups with a view to offering them a home. I also deal with phone calls from people who have lost their dogs. It's amazing how many people do not have a collar and tag on their dog, even though it's the law! The usual excuse is ''Oh it fell off a couple of days ago!''

'Some puppies may need some medication of some kind during the day and they all need lots of love and cuddles.

'When someone decides they would like a pup, they fill out a questionnaire and we have a chat about it. If they appear to be suitable owners they can reserve a pup and they are then ''home-checked'' so that we can be as sure as we can that the pup will be going into a suitable home environment. If everything looks good they come back and collect the pup.

'When a puppy is brought in it is immediately wormed, vaccinated and de-flead. We can house up to 100 puppies at one time. The vet comes in once a week and sees any animals that require attention.

'The best bits of my job are playing with the puppies and seeing them go out to loving (and hopefully permanent) homes.

'There is a down side; it can be smelly, cold and noisy and you can become very cynical towards people as you have to deal with many ignorant and uncaring people. It's hard when you have to deal with the return of a dog when you know it's not the dog's fault at all. The low wages are also a negative point.

'There are some perhaps surprising elements to my job; I frequently write poetry for the dogs to try to help them get homes, and once a week cable television comes here and we do a parade of dogs needing homes. We are also all trained to microchip the dogs and I also engrave dog discs!

'We work from 9am to 5pm and have alternate weekends off but we have to work over Christmas and New Year — although we all get on so well that even if I was not working I would still spend Christmas here. On most Bank Holidays we work half days and have four weeks holiday per year.

'My ambition is to one day have a kennels of my own, either boarding or rescue. I would not breed dogs — not after seeing the results here of over-breeding. I did leave here four years ago to be a veterinary nurse but I was back within a year. For me, this job is so much more rewarding.'

THE NATIONAL CANINE DEFENCE LEAGUE

The National Canine Defence League is famous for its slogan, 'A dog is for life . . . not just for Christmas.' It was founded in 1891 in London to protect dogs from torture and ill-usage of every kind. Originally, there were 116 centres in Britain. These centres were run by members from their own homes, to which local owners brought their dogs when they needed help. This work eventually led to the dogs' homes and clinics that exist today.

There are now thirteen rescue centres and two affiliated kennels throughout the country based at Dumfries, West Calder (Scotland), Darlington, Leeds, Whitby, Kenilworth, Attleborough, Shoreham, Farringdon, Newbury, Ilfracombe, Bridgend, Evesham, Shrewsbury, Ballymena (N. Ireland).

The NCDL has a policy of non-destruction — a dog is only put to sleep for humane reasons. All bitches are neutered before going to a home and the majority of males are castrated.

During 1993, a total of 8,858 dogs were cared for at NCDL kennels, but with two new centres opened in 1994, the projected annual figure is now likely to be 10,000 dogs. As well as the dogs that are re-homed, some 300 or so are long term residents which, for one reason or another, have proved difficult to re-home. These dogs are supported via the NCDL's Sponsored Dog Scheme. The Centres care for up to 200 dogs at any one time and the following example, Wickhamford NCDL kennels in Worcestershire, costs around £3,000 per week to operate. This particular centre houses up to 180 dogs at a time.

The centres are run locally so far as decisions regarding feed, opening times and staff rotas are concerned but all centres are managed at a national level by a field secretary, implementing policies set up by a board of trustees. The League relies entirely upon membership, legacies and donations for its income.

Kennel assistants
These deal with the day to day running and cleaning of the kennels in addition to dealing with emergencies (*eg* dog fights), dogs coming in, showing customers around the premises and dealing with their requests to walk dogs of their choice, adoption, special diets, administering drugs and assisting the veterinary surgeon. Assistants work a five and a half day week on a shift system, with one weekend off in three.

Qualities looked for
Experience, such as voluntary work for a welfare charity, or at a boarding kennels, is not essential, though is useful. Staff must be caring, dedicated, patient and polite and able to deal with stressful situations. Applicants are considered from the school leaving age upwards.

Job functions at Wickhamford kennels
Manager, assistant manageress, administrator, 10 full time kennel assistants, and voluntary helpers.

Voluntary positions
1. Assisting with kennels/ground work.
2. Dog walking.
3. Fund raising.

Limited work experience placements are possible at all of the centres. Contact the local Manager for details.

Vacancies are advertised in the local papers and job centres. Senior positions are advertised internally and then in *Our Dogs/Dog World* and in the national press.

Further information

Details of membership, junior membership, newsletters and events can be obtained from: National Canine Defence League, 19-26 Wakley Street, Angel, Islington, London N1. Tel: (0171) 388 0137.

A celebration of the first 100 years of the National Canine Defence League, published by NCDL, is available entitled *A Dog is for Life* by Peter Ballard.

BLUE CROSS

In 1897 the Blue Cross, then called 'Our Dumb Friends League', was founded in London. Its aim was to encourage kindness to all animals. The first Animals Hospital was opened in London in 1906.

During the First World War (1914-1918) tens of thousands of horses and dogs were used on the front line alongside British and French soldiers. The League's Blue Cross veterinary posts were established in France, treating 2,800 horses in the first year alone, and so the name Blue Cross became established.

Today the Blue Cross finds loving homes for abandoned, stray and unwanted animals and provides care for thousands of sick, injured, unwanted and abandoned animals. It has three hospitals and a London clinic, eleven adoption centres, a horse protection scheme and a head office at the Burford field centre.

Job functions

Adoption centres

The centres are situated at: Burford, Bromsgrove, Cambridge, Chalfont St Peter, Felixstowe, Kimpton Bottom (Herts), Southampton, Northiam (Sussex), Thirsk, Tiverton and Torquay.

Centre manager

The position of centre manager requires extensive experience in animal welfare. Duties include supervising the running of the centre, staff management, implementing Blue Cross policy, advising members of the public wishing to adopt animals, fund raising, public relations, administration and book-keeping.

Deputy centre manager
The deputy centre manager runs the centre in the absence of the manager. The duties are similar to those of manager but with the support and guidance of the manager.

Animal welfare assistants
There are normally between three and seven animal welfare assistants at each centre. Prior experience caring for animals is preferred, but not essential. Applicants must have a flexible attitude and have a dedicated approach. The duties include the day to day care of the animals, cleaning kennels, grooming, walking dogs, feeding.

Blue Cross Hospitals
In 1992 52,565 animals were treated in Blue Cross hospitals where care is provided for animals belonging to those on low incomes. Thirteen veterinary surgeons are employed at the various veterinary hospitals.

All Blue Cross Hospitals are approved training centres for veterinary nursing.

Other job functions include: radiographer, laboratory technicians, almoner night superintendents and ambulance drivers.

Head Office
The Head Office co-ordinates the work of the organisation and is divided into the following departments: marketing, administration & finance, animal welfare and the horse protection scheme. The veterinary department is based at Victoria.

There are limited YTS and work experience placements available at Blue Cross Adoption Centres and hospitals. Applications should be made in writing to the appropriate centre manager, giving full course details where applicable.

Positions within Blue Cross are advertised in the local or national press.

All information is taken from the information leaflet *Careers with Blue Cross* which is available on application from the Blue Cross Head Office, Shilton Road, Burford, Oxon OX18 4PF. Tel: (01993) 822651.

THE DOGS' HOME BATTERSEA

Battersea is the oldest dogs' home in the world. Opened in 1860 by Mrs Mary Tealby it was then called 'The Temporary Home for Lost

& Starving Dogs' and was situated in Holloway, north London. The
newly established charity moved south in 1871 to the present site
between two railway lines near Battersea Power Station.

The Home takes in strays, lost and abandoned dogs from the
greater metropolitan area, in other words, within the M25. Animals
are held for the statutory seven days to see if they are going to be
reclaimed and then if possible they are re-homed. Sadly, only 25%
of dogs are re-claimed. In 1993, 10,845 dogs were received into the
home, plus 1,384 cats.

On arrival all dogs are checked over by one of a team of veterinary nurses and are inoculated, de-flead and wormed. After seven
days, if not reclaimed, depending on the dog's state of health and
temperament, the animal will be available for re-homing. Some dogs
are suitable for re-homing immediately but some require months of
care to restore them back to good health.

The Home has a country annex — Bell Mead Kennels in Old
Windsor (see page 28) which can act as an overflow, but more often
as a convalescent and maternity home.

In order to try and provide the best environment for the dogs and
cats during their stay at Battersea, a huge building programme is
being implemented which should be complete by the end of 1995.
The new accommodation will consist of two four-storey kennel
blocks and a visitor and reception block.

Battersea has a Junior Members Club open to anyone under the
age of 18. This gives an account of the Homes' activities through an
annual club magazine. Details from: The Junior Members Club, The
Dogs' Home Battersea, 4 Battersea Park Road, London SW8 4AA.

Staff jobs

Battersea employs over a hundred full time staff plus the staff at
Bell Mead (15 full time plus part time staff).

The staff are divided into the following categories:

● managerial

● administration

● kennel hands (including 4 deputy supervisors and 3 supervisors)

● rehoming staff (including 3 supervisors)

● transport staff (including a head of department)

- reception staff (including a head of department)

- customer liaison staff (including a head of department)

- home visitors (part time)

- maintenance staff

- veterinary staff (including one veterinary surgeon and twelve nurses)

- night staff

There is a structured career ladder for staff which means that it is perfectly possible for someone starting as a kennel hand to develop on through to managerial level. The staff turnover is quite low, with many staff having worked at the Home for many years.

Kennel hands

Kennel hands deal with the day to day care of the animals. 'On spec' applications for kennel hand positions are kept on a register and when around six positions become available those applicants from the register that appear to be suitable will be invited to an interview. As with all job functions at Battersea, candidates are interviewed initially by the director general and then by the other managers informally. Of those who attend the interviews, six will be selected; they then complete a week long induction course.

On successful completion of the induction course the kennel hands do a three month probationary period. While they then work up through the kennel hand grades they study the Small Animal Care Course (NVQ 2).

Minimum age
18 years

Qualities looked for
An affinity with animals is a bonus but not mandatory. Applicants must be literate and numerate, not too sentimental and must be able to display a willingness to change and a willingness to learn. A team worker is essential.

Kennel hands, if they so wish and are considered suitable, are able to move up the career ladder to one of the following job functions:

Rehoming staff
These deal with the public, interviewing potential owners and then matching them with the dogs. They do a 'dealing with the public' course and a behaviour course.

Drivers
These need to be knowledgeable about handling dogs as they collect them, often in a frightened and/or in poor physical condition, from the police stations.

Customer liaison staff
These deal with newly homed dogs and cats and their owners.

Other job functions
Receptionists
They are in the front line of dealing with the public and have to be able to answer many and varied questions about dogs.

Managerial, clerical and administration positions
These are advertised in the national press.

Veterinary staff
These, or positions where veterinary experience is preferred, are advertised in the *Vet Record*. The Home is an approved training centre for veterinary nurses.

Internal courses other than those already mentioned include reception courses and 2 levels of management.

Limited work experience placements are available with the Home but need to be booked up to a year in advance.

Further information
The Dogs' Home Battersea, 4 Battersea Park Road, London SW8 4AA. Tel: (0171) 622 3626.

WOOD GREEN ANIMAL SHELTERS

In 1924 a shelter was opened in Wood Green, North London, for stray, neglected and unwanted animals. By the early 1930s, Dr Margaret Young had become involved with the shelter and then developed it to the stage whereby it could offer treatment and care to animals and renew hope for their owners.

Today, the London Shelter still provides daily clinic sessions, offering free treatments for animals whose owners are suffering financial hardship. During the 1950s a larger shelter was opened in Heydon, Herts and later the Margaret Young Home for Animals was opened on a 50-acre site at Godmanchester, Cambridgeshire. This site has facilities to care for many different species of animals from hamsters to llamas. Around 80% of animals are rehomed and there are also some permanent residents who are sponsored by members of the public and are visited regularly.

The College of Animal Welfare, which is run by Wood Green Animal Shelters, is on the site of Godmanchester and is part of the Kings Bush Centre, which also has an arena and banqueting and conference suite. The college runs courses all through the year including kennel & cattery management, animal wardens, animal first aid and veterinary nursing.

Job functions
Wood Green employs 215 staff divided between:

- animal care attendant/officers
- supervisory staff
- veterinary surgeons
- nurses and trainees
- home visitors
- dog wardens
- administration and marketing officers
- maintenance

Qualifications
A good education and willingness to learn. NVQ levels 1 & 2 can be attained within Wood Green Animal Shelters. Staff follow formal training schemes within the organisation.

Qualities
A desire to work and care for animals.
Minimum age: 16 years.

Vacancies
Vacancies are advertised in the local press and internally.

Further information
Enquiries should be made to: The Personnel Officer, Wood Green Animal Shelters, London Road, Godmanchester, Huntingdon, Cambridgeshire PE18 8LJ. Tel: (01480) 830014.

Details of courses can be obtained from: The College of Animal Welfare, Kings Bush Farm, Godmanchester, Cambridgeshire PE18 8LJ.

The Critters Club
This club is aimed at young people who are keen to be involved with the Shelter's work and enjoy a variety of activities and events organised by Wood Green throughout the year.

Details from: The Critters Club, Wood Green Animal Shelters, Heydon, Royston, Hertfordshire SG8 8PN.

6
'Hands Off' Careers with Dogs

If you do not want to work physically with dogs, there are several other ways you can enjoy a career in the dog world. In this chapter we will discuss three of them:

● journalism
● pet bereavement counselling
● The Kennel Club

JOURNALISM

There are a growing number of specialist dog magazines, journals, annuals and papers that provide opportunities for journalists at all levels.

Journalism is a career that people may train for in general terms, before specialising in a field of particular interest to them. Working as a freelance offers a great opportunity for working part time and/or from home.

The job

A journalist may seek out, research and write newsworthy articles for all kinds of publications: newspapers, magazines and periodicals and even television and radio. It can be a high pressure job with deadlines to be met and often requires reactions to news stories at short notice.

In general terms, journalism can be divided into these three main areas:

● reporters — the people who write the articles having done the appropriate research.

● sub editors — who correct grammar, punctuation and spelling and make the articles more readable. They write the headlines and reduce or enlarge articles to fit the intended paper/magazine if necessary.

- editors — who are responsible for the overall policy and content of the publication.

Training
University
You can study journalism at university and use your qualification to help you get a job after graduating.

Pre-entry
This is a one year college course run by the National Council for the Training of Journalists. It covers law, public administration, journalism and shorthand. Exams are taken during the NCTJ training period which culminate in a final exam and if passed a NCTJ Certificate is awarded.
Minimum qualification: two A levels.

Direct entry
You can serve an apprenticeship with a provincial paper and combine it with a NCTJ course during the first two years.

Qualities required
Observation skills, accuracy, patience, willingness to travel, confidence, preparedness to work long and irregular hours, a team worker, self motivation, excellent secretarial skills.

The appropriate qualifications can certainly help to make you stand out from the crowd. An advertisement for a journalist post advertised in the media section of the *Guardian* can produce around 400 applicants, so you really do need to shine out to be noticed.

Smaller organisations tend to give a good grounding. You would probably be required to do more than one task and your willingness to carry out menial tasks should be pointed out in your application.

Another way into the industry is to become an editorial secretary, making sure that you are adaptable and as indispensable as possible. You can then work up from there, for example to proof reading and other basic editorial duties.

Useful contacts
Chartered Institute of Journalists, 2 Dock Offices, Surrey Quays Road, London SE16 2XL. Tel: (0171) 252 1187.

National Council for the Training of Journalists, Latton Bush Centre, Southern Way, Harlow, Essex CM18 7BH. Tel: (01279) 430009.

Specialising in canine publications

You may be able to break into the work of journalism without going through apprenticeships. If you are competent and knowledgeable about your subject it may be possible to freelance, that is to write articles for magazines and papers and to submit them in the hope that someone will buy them. It is always a good idea to contact the editor first so you can discuss your idea and get an opinion as to whether it would fit the magazine's requirements. Always study copies of the publication beforehand to acquaint yourself with its particular style.

Many of the breed clubs produce internal magazines/newsletters, which can provide an opportunity for you to build up your confidence about submitting material. As with all newsletter type publications, the editor is often quite hard pressed to find regular and interesting articles, but that is not an excuse for sending in poor quality work. It is unlikely that you would be paid for such articles but it would help to get your name known and give you good practice. The magazine will also need an editor — a good opportunity to practise your editorial skills. It will also help you build up your CV, not only because it will prove your credibility for writing but it will stand out that you are so interested in the subject that you have been willing to do it voluntarily.

Having specialised in a given area there is often limited scope for promotion. Having reached the point of editor many journalists stay there for the rest of their working lives. Ambitious people could well find this frustrating. If you applied for the position of editor of a national magazine you would probably find yourself competing with qualified career journalists rather than dog enthusiasts.

Jobs advertised

Careers offices, national press, local press, specialist magazines tend to advertise within their own publication as their readers will already be familiar with their style.

Journalism can prove to be a good stepping stone for moving on into public relations (which tends to be better paid). Many large pet food manufacturers, for example, employ PR companies.

A day in the life of . . .

Beverley Cuddy, Editor, 'Dogs Today'
'I first came into journalism ten years ago. I had no formal training

as a journalist but was fortunate enough to be offered a job with *Dog World* (a weekly paper), subediting the show reports after working as a reporter for their rival, *Our Dogs*. I moved on to be the Kennel Club's Information Officer. I applied for the Editor's position at *Dogs Today* before it was launched; at that time it was owned by the *Daily Mail*. After two years we had a management buy-out and have been publishing it ourselves for a year now. We have recently been presented with the Periodical Association Award for Small Publisher of the Year — not bad for our first year!

'*Dogs Today* is currently Britain's top selling pet magazine with a circulation of 65,000 and it is still in its growth period. I enjoy working on magazines in preference to papers as the papers were show-orientated and there was less room for creativity.

'In our office we all need to be multi-skilled. When copy comes in it is keyed into the computer. It then goes on to be subbed before being sent on to the designer. The designer sends the page proofs back to us for proofing.

'We have so many unsolicited articles coming in that sadly we can only use less than 1%. I try to go out myself and cover a couple of stories per issue rather than just waiting for press releases. That way we get a different angle on the stories from everyone else.

'The best bits of the job are the day the magazine comes in from the printers, when we see the colour proofs for the first time. I also enjoy the photo shoot for the front cover. It can be stressful and tiring but it's another opportunity to be creative, and it's good fun as well.

'The worst bits are the bad pay and the boring business side — doing the VAT returns, chasing bad debts and so on.

'My routine varies from day to day, but usually the post that arrives first thing will determine how my day will go. I juggle with what's in the post — comments and queries from readers, tip offs about local stories, and also deal with the many telephone calls from contributors, advertising queries, and press contacts. I also need to brief the illustrators and photographers. In a small office like ours it is very important that you are able to concentrate while others are dealing with calls and also, very importantly, be aware of the needs of the other people working with you. We normally work 9am to 6 ish, but longer if our deadline is close.'

PET BEREAVEMENT COUNSELLORS

Some people have great difficulty accepting the loss of their pet, and may then contact a pet bereavement counsellor.

Counselling is defined by the British Association of Counsellors as 'engaging in counselling when you occupy regularly or temporarily the role of counsellor and you offer or agree explicitly to offer time, attention and respect to another person or persons temporarily in the role of client. The task of counselling is to give the client an opportunity to explore, discover and clarify ways of living more resourcefully and toward greater well-being.'

Many bereavement counsellors are accredited counsellors who specialise in pet bereavement. Pet bereavement counselling alone is unlikely to provide a living wage for someone; however the skills can be useful in other jobs such as veterinary nurses, who are often in the front line. Most pet bereavement counselling is done by telephone or letter, which makes it rather difficult to make a charge.

Very often, the type of person who requires bereavement counselling has underlying problems which need to be identified. Where appropriate, the client needs to be helped with those problems or referred on to whatever specialist help is needed, so good general counselling skills as well as an understanding of other types of therapy is essential.

Many counsellors become interested in counselling having been on the receiving end for some reason. It is important that their own counselling has been completed so that, in this particular field for example, past bereavement does not cause distress having been awakened by someone else's problem. You will not be of any use to anyone if you are distressed yourself.

Training

There are, at present, no courses designed specifically for pet bereavement but there are plenty of general counselling courses available, some through RELATE and others at local colleges. Some lead to Certificates or Diplomas in Counselling, some are part time, some full time and certified courses usually last for about two years.

A directory of recognised courses is available in the BAC publication *Training in Counselling & Psychotherapy: A Directory* available from BAC, 1 Regent Place, Rugby CV21 2PJ. Information line: (01788) 578328.

There are many 'introduction to counselling' courses available which can give a good insight into the role of the counsellor. They can help you to decide if it really is for you. It should be emphasised again that pet bereavement counselling would only be a small part of your job as a counsellor, and that you must be comfortable with the other aspects of it as well.

Counsellors must be very open minded, non-judgmental, strong minded but sympathetic, good listeners and able to empathise with the client.

THE KENNEL CLUB

Perhaps one of the best known organisations in the dog world is that of The Kennel Club, founded in 1873 to be a controlling body legislating on canine matters. At that time, dog shows were becoming popular in Victorian England, especially as the railways were bringing the whole country within reach. In 1900 nearly 30 championship shows were held and the smaller shows were becoming more popular. These days the number of shows increases annually, perhaps 4,000 a year. The most famous dog show in the world, Crufts, is run by The Kennel Club.

The role of The Kennel Club today is, as it has always been, to look after the interests of pedigree dogs in all aspects of survival, showing, agility, field trials, and obedience. The only areas not involved are greyhound racing and sheepdog training, each of which have their own regulating bodies. Kennel Club staff are not policy makers but the 'civil service' of the dog world, all decisions being made by the General Committee. The Club is funded by registrations and licence fees.

The first objective in the rules and regulations of the Club has always been 'to promote in every way, the general improvement of dogs'. This includes classification of the breeds, registration of pedigrees, transfers, the licensing of shows, the framing and enforcing of Kennel Club Rules, the awarding of Challenge, Champion and other certificates, the registration of associations, clubs and societies and the publication of an annual *Stud Book* and monthly *Kennel Gazette*.

The Kennel Club *Stud Book* was one of the earliest undertakings of the Kennel Club; it contains records of shows and data relating to dogs which have been successful in Championship shows during the previous year. Originally, to be eligible for inclusion into the *Stud Book*, societies had to adopt a code of ten rules which related to the shows. These days the guarantors of a show have to sign an undertaking to hold and conduct the show under and in accordance with the rules and regulations of The Kennel Club.

The *Kennel Gazette*, a monthly magazine, was first published by The Kennel Club in 1880 and has been published every month since that date. It is available from larger newsagents or on subscription from the Club.

Today, all 110 employees in the various departments of The Kennel Club are based at Clarges Street, in central London.

Jobs in The Kennel Club

- Chief Executive/Secretary

- Senior Managers

- Managers

- Departmental Managers

- Editorial — Editor/Assistant Editor/Production Assistant

- Secretarial — secretaries/PA/executive assistant/clerk typists/ typists/audio typist/administrators

- Clerical — telephone/enquiry/processing/data control/post/ photocopying/research

- Catering — steward/cook/waiting staff/bar person/dining room staff

- Administration — for field trials/judges/switchboard/reception support

- PR — External Affairs Officer/information officers/Crufts/ librarian/library assistant

- Financial — accounts/clerks

- Computer — technical support/VDU operators

The offices of senior management are the equivalent to directors in commercial organisations. Some managers started working at The Kennel Club as clerks/secretaries and worked their way up.

Crufts Dog Show

Crufts Dog Show, which celebrated its centenary in 1991 has been run by The Kennel Club since 1948, when the Club purchased the right to do so from Charles Crufts' widow. The Show is now held in

Birmingham over four days in Spring each year. Some 20,000 dogs are exhibited; it attracts a crowd of 90,000 people, including visitors from all over the world. Most Kennel Club staff are involved in the show in some way.

The Kennel Club library

This is the leading canine library in Europe and one of the principal libraries in the world. It is open to the public on Tuesdays, Wednesdays and Thursday from 9.30am to 4.30pm (by appointment only).

Library staff turnover is generally low.

Vacancies are advertised in various publications depending upon the type of vacancy; senior positions may be advertised in *The Times*, *The Guardian* and *The Telegraph*. Clerical vacancies may be advertised in *The Evening Standard*, *Dog World* and *Our Dogs*. On spec applications are kept on file and are considered as and when a vacancy arises. Employment agencies are also sometimes used for specific job functions, for example VDU operators.

Qualities/qualifications required

It is useful for potential applicants to have some knowledge of the dog world, so as to understand the terminology, but this is not essential. In fact, there are some positions where staff find they can no longer show their own dogs because of their role within The Kennel Club.

- You need a general education standard to GCSE and A level, including English. Good keyboard skills (fast and accurate), plus shorthand and/or audio skills and numeracy skills are required for secretaries.

- Customer care is very important. With an average of 4,000 telephone calls and 5,500 items of post arriving every week, good communication skills, a good eye for detail, willingness and an enthusiastic manner are essential.

- Limited work experience placements are possible.

Further information

All enquiries to: The Personnel Manager, The Kennel Club, 1-5 Clarges Street, Piccadilly, London W1Y 8AB. Tel: (0171) 493 6651.

7
Working in Education & Research

Here we will look at some of the other possibilities for careers involving dogs, for example in education and research. In this chapter we will discuss the work of two particular organisations:

- Waltham Centre for Pet Nutrition
- The Animal Welfare & Human/Animal Interactions Group

Education and research covers a very wide field, from pharmaceutical companies to university departments.

This particular section concentrates on the Waltham Centre for Pet Nutrition, a renowned centre of excellence, both in quality of staff and working conditions, and the Animal Welfare & Human-Animal Interactions Group at the University of Cambridge. Obviously conditions and practices will vary greatly from organisation to organisation depending on the type of research, company values, and educational setting. Despite that, this section should still give an insight into this part of the industry. Some jobs will be hands on, some hands off.

Job vacancies are often advertised in the national press and *The New Scientist*, or *Nature Magazine*.

WALTHAM CENTRE FOR PET NUTRITION

WALTHAM Centre for Pet Nutrition provides the science behind Mars Petcare products worldwide (Mars are well known for their confectionery ranges but also have subsidiary companies dealing in main meals, drinks, and electronics as well as petcare). The WALTHAM Centre is located in Leicestershire and there are other WALTHAM Centres around the world, such as the WALTHAM Centre for Equine Nutrition and Care, based in Germany.

WCPN is the base of WALTHAM worldwide. It is the world's

leading authority on pet care and nutrition, carrying out studies into the nutrition, behaviour and husbandry of companion animals, all of which fits in with the overall aim of WALTHAM, which is to improve the health and well being of pet animals.

The state-of-the-art facilities at WCPN are exceptional. The resident pets (some 250 dogs and 450 cats) enjoy a high quality of life. They are housed in purpose built accommodation, and looked after by highly trained staff whose duties revolve around ensuring that the pets receive all the attention, training and care required to keep them fit, happy and healthy.

Sixteen breeds of dog are kept at the centre, from Yorkshire terriers to Irish wolfhounds. Puppies are assigned to a pet care associate or kennel person at eight weeks of age until homed. During this period, a puppy will have received as much socialising as possible to ensure that it will settle happily into normal family life.

Studies are non-invasive ensuring that all the animals are healthy and happy. Work is carried out by experts in their field. The advanced computer systems routinely handle and process over 26,000 items of data each week.

Job functions

Pet care associates
The role of a PCA is to ensure that the animals in his or her care receive the exercise, attention and care that they require. All PCAs are responsible for one particular group of animals — breeding queens, puppies *etc*. However they are all trained and expected to work in all areas.

The pet care associates are responsible for a variety of duties:

1. One area of husbandry/cleaning kennels.

2. Some PCAs run the dog training programme and are responsible for matching the dogs to the handlers and ensuring that they are getting enough stimulation for their development.

3. Some PCAs are responsible for the clipping/trimming of the dogs and teaching others the skills required. They make sure that all the dogs are groomed regularly and that the grooming/clipping equipment is properly maintained.

4. Kitten and puppy rehoming.

5. Looking after stores, and logging deliveries.

6. Assisting the veterinary surgeons on visits to the centre.

7. Carrying out dog and cat socialisation programmes, especially between birth and twelve weeks of age.

8. Liaison with pet care technicians.

Qualities required

● Experience of caring for large numbers of animals.

● A Small Animal Care Certificate is advantageous.

● Knowledge/experience in another related area is preferable, *eg* clipping, dog training. This knowledge will be utilised within the centre.

● Some GCSEs, including Maths and English.

Vacancies
Positions are advertised in the local press/dog press/cat press.

Training
This is dependent upon the individual's needs. Most training is in-house but external courses can be taken in order to meet others and learn new skills.

Due to the very good working conditions and job satisfaction within the organisation, vacancies are filled very quickly.

Kennel persons
Kennel persons are trained in-house by senior kennel persons for every single task, no matter how simple. Sixty per cent of the kennel person's time is spent cleaning housing; the rest is spent exercising, grooming, bathing, socialising and training dogs.

Qualities required
Enthusiasm, a team worker, a love of dogs and cats, some previous experience.

Vacancies
Kennel persons are recruited from adverts in the local press.

Pet care technicians

The pet care technicians work closely with the project scientists and nutritionists. Pet care technicians are responsible for the implementation of nutritional feeding studies and the care and welfare of the dogs and cats, plus the specific responsibility for planning and co-ordination of trials and analysis of the results.

Qualifications needed

Degree in biological science. Post qualification research experience is advantageous but not necessary. Applicants should be numerate and capable of handling computer data and presenting findings convincingly. Applicants should also be self motivated and good team workers.

Project scientists

Project scientists are responsible for the planning and implementation of studies.

Qualifications needed

Good honours degree in biological or food science, followed by at least three years in a relevant research environment; creativity and ability to take on responsibility.

There are also nutritionists, behaviourists and biologists who each require similar qualifications to project scientists.

On spec applications are not accepted for any of these jobs.

Working in university research departments

Animal Welfare & Human/Animal Interactions Group, Cambridge University

The Animal Welfare & Human Animal Interactions Group is part of the Department of Clinical Veterinary Medicine at Cambridge University. The Department teaches veterinary students and carries out research to advance veterinary science.

It is usual for universities to have research groups within their departments. These are largely funded by government agencies, companies or organisations which are interested in a particular area of research, for example food and pharmaceutical companies or major charities. The research staff in these groups are post-doctoral research associates, students studying for their doctorates, and assistants. Some of the research students come to Britain from overseas and return to their own country after obtaining their PhD.

The aim of the Cambridge group is to investigate how to improve the welfare of farm animals, companion animals, other animals used by man, and wild animals. A further aim is to study how people affect domestic animals and how these animals affect people. In 1994 the group had sixteen members of whom six were involved in studies of dogs and cats. During research into such things as puppy testing and specific behaviours in dogs there is a lot of contact with pet owners. Other studies are carried out at kennels, animal shelters or dog training centres.

8
Other Career Possibilities

It is possible for someone with a head for business, plenty of imagination and a desire to work in an area close to their heart to turn their skills or expertise into doing just that. The following case study is just such an example. Others include canine photography, painting, sculpting, producing accessories, designing kennels, canine taxis, chiropractor, reflexology, and touch therapy.

Do you have skills that you could adapt in this way?

PAWS & CO (DENISE LEFFMAN)

Denise began Paws & Co after adopting a scruffy black mongrel (called Paws) from a rescue home. Unable to find any good quality, attractive collars and leads for Paws in London, Denise, a former Marks & Spencer's buyer, found what she was looking for whilst on holiday in America; she knew that if she couldn't find what she was looking for in that country then it probably didn't exist. Recognising the fact that if high-quality, exclusive products were what she wanted, she realised that others may well feel the same way. After some careful sleuthing, Denise was able to find the company who made Paws' collar and put forward a proposition that she would represent them in the UK and Europe. Paws & Co took off when Denise showed samples of the goods to Harrods and Selfridges in London, who immediately placed orders.

Fun in a very important word at Paws & Co; Denise has a strong belief that pet ownership should be fun.

Paws & Co is a small business supplying the needs of a few dog owners as it only sells very upmarket, high-quality goods to a small number of stores. The range includes beautiful hand painted pottery bowls, 'Jingle Bells' collars for Christmas, coats for winter and rain wear, collars and leads, cotton bandanna scarves containing a herbal flea repellent, solid brass, gold-plated identity tags in various shapes, flashing collars for night-time-winter walks, teddy bear toys and carrying bags which could easily double as sports bags.

Actually tracking down the goods in the first instance can be something of an adventure. For instance, the pottery dishes are made by a lady whom Denise found at a craft fair in a village in Oregon. At the other extreme, Denise also attends huge pet trade fairs in the USA, where manufacturers who produce hundreds of products display their wares. Out of perhaps a hundred or more items produced by any one manufacturer, Denise will probably only pick one or two products which are good enough for Paws & Co.

Denise's experience as a buyer has taught her many things, including how to choose the products to give a balanced range. She uses her skills not only in finding the right products but also in negotiating deals, arranging shipping and customs details, purchasing foreign currency, finding the right buyers, making deliveries and general office work.

Paws & Co has customers in Paris and an agent in the south and south west of France as well as the London based business. However, Denise adds that deliberately aiming her products at a very limited market means that her type of business would not provide a large income, but she is doing all the things she enjoys and is lucky enough to call it work.

Appendix 1
The Kennel Club
Junior Organisation

The Kennel Club Junior Organisation has the following aims;

1. To encourage young people between the ages of 8 and 18 to take an interest in the care and training of dogs and to enjoy all activities connected with dogs.
2. To promote courtesy, sportsmanship, loyalty and self-discipline.
3. To develop a sense of responsibility in canine activities.

ANNUAL EVENTS

Many annual events take place, including;

*   The Agility Dog of the Year Competition
*   KCJO Crufts Agility Competition
*   Show Handler of the Year Competition
*   Obedience competitions
*   KCJO Stakes Classes and Final
*   Annual Quiz Competition
*   National Camp

There are other activities including regional events. These may consist of various talks on breeds, rare breeds, feeding and nutrition, puppy care, aspects of the veterinary profession and demonstrations and instruction in dog obedience and agility.

MEMBERSHIP

Open to those between the ages of 8 and 18. An application form is available from the Kennel Club at the address below. There is an annual subscription of £5.00 and £3.00 for brothers and sisters who wish to join. In return you will receive your membership badge and handbook, the name and address of your regional organiser as well as future events.

You do not need to own a dog yourself to join, you just need to be interested in dogs and their care and training.

The Kennel Club
1-5 Clarges Street
Piccadilly
London
W1Y 8AB.
Tel: (0171) 493 6651.

All the above information has been reprinted with the kind permission of The Kennel Club.

Appendix 2
National Vocational Qualifications

National Vocational Qualifications (NVQs) are awarded for competent performance in animal care activities and are normally assessed in the work place. They are awarded for doing the job to the standards set by industry and established bodies. More details about NVQs can be obtained from: NCVQ, 222 Euston Road, London NW1 2BZ.

ANIMAL CARE NVQs

NVQs in Animal Care are available at 2 levels;

Animal Care Level 1

001 Maintaining the provision of food and water to the animals

002 Assisting in maintaining animal accommodation

003 Contributing to the maintenance of animal hygiene, health and safety

004 Assisting in the moving, exercising and restraining of animals

005 Maintaining personal hygiene, health and safety

006 Liaising with callers and colleagues

007 Communication

Animal Care Level 2

008 Handling stock

009 Providing food and water for animals

010 Maintaining animal accommodation

011 Moving, exercising and restraining animals

012 Maintaining personal hygiene, health and safety

013 Maintaining health of animals

014 Maintaining wellbeing of animals

015 Gathering and providing information

016 Creating and maintaining business relationships

017 Reception

018 Record keeping

These standards are current as of the publishing date of this book and are subject to change.

Success in any one unit is recognised on a Record of Achievement and success in all units at Level 1 or 2 is recognised on a certificate which is endorsed by the National Council for Vocational Qualifications.

ASSESSMENT CENTRES

Assessment is carried out at an approved training centre; a list of centres can be obtained from the National Examinations Board for Agriculture, Horticulture and Allied Industries (NEBAHAI). Tel: (0171) 278 2468.

CONTACT

The Animal Care Industry Lead Body, c/o The Education Department, Wood Green Animal Shelter, King's Bush Farm, London Road, Huntingdon, Cambs PE18 8LJ.

Glossary

Air-scent cone. Pattern of wind blown scent distribution.

Anaesthesia. Artificially induced insensitivity to pain usually achieved by the administration of gases or drugs.

Bacteriology. Scientific study of bacteria.

Biochemistry. Chemistry of living things.

Canine. Relating to dogs.

Congress. A formal meeting of delegates for discussion.

Continuation training. The practising of established skills and development beyond basic training.

Customs collection. Division of the country by Customs & Excise.

Dual task dogs. Specialist dogs trained for more than one purpose.

Empathy. The power of identifying oneself mentally with and so understanding a person/animal.

Entire. Unneutered.

Ethology. The science of animal behaviour.

Husbandry. The business of a farmer.

Induction course. Introductory course.

Microbiology. Biology of microscopic organisms.

Nutritionists. Expert in foods and their nutritional values.

Olfactory system. Physical capacity for smelling.

Orthopaedics. Process for curing deformities arising from disease/injury.

Parasitology. Study of parasites.

Passive dogs. Dogs trained to indicate the presence of a particular substance on a person.

Pathology. Study of disease or abnormalities.

Pharmacology. Science of drugs.

Physiology. The science of living organisms and their parts.

Pool trained dogs. Dogs trained by trainers at a dog training centre as opposed to those trained together with the handler.

Probationary period. A period of testing the character or abilities of a new employee.

Radiography. The science of X rays.

Socialisation. Systematically ensuring that puppies learn to relate properly to people and other dogs.

Specialist dogs. Dogs trained for a specific task.

Tracking. Utilisation of the dog's capacity to ground scent via its olfactory system.

Zoology. Scientific study of animals.

Further Reading

BOOKS

Absent Friend, M. & L. Lee (Henson)*

Advanced Gundog Training: Practical Fieldwork and Competition, Martin Deeley (Crowood Press).

Allbreed Dog Grooming Guide, Sam Kohn & Catherine Goldstein (Arco).

Barking Up the Right Tree: Breeding, Rearing and Training Guide Dogs, Derek Freeman (Ringwood).

The Behaviour of Dogs and Cats, APBC, edited by John Fisher (Stanley Paul).*

The Behavioural Effects of Canine Castration, edited by David Appleby (Dog Help).*

Black's Veterinary Dictionary, Geoffrey West (A. & C. Black).

Book of Dogs (Readers Digest).

Canine Terminology, Harold Spira (Harper & Row).

Do Dogs Need Shrinks, Peter Neville (Sidgwick & Jackson).*

Dog and Cat Nutrition, edited by Andrew Edney (Pergamon Press).

Dog Breeding: A Guide to Mating & Whelping, Kay White (Bartholomew).

A Dog is for Life: The First 100 Years of the National Canine Defence League, Peter Ballard (NCDL).

The Dog Law Handbook, Godfrey Sandys-Winsch (Shaw & Sons).

Dog Watching, Desmond Morris (Jonathan Cape).

Dog Wise, John Fisher (Souvenir Press).*

The Dog's Mind, Bruce Fogle (Pelham).

Doglopedia, Jim Evans and Kay White (Henson).

Good Behaviour Guide, David Appleby (Dog Help).*

Grooming Dogs for Profit, Charlotte Gold (Howell Book House).

How to Have a Happy Puppy, David Appleby (Dog Help).*

How to Teach an Old Dog New Tricks, Ian Dunbar.

Jones Animal Nursing, edited by Dick Lane (Pergamon Press). Official textbook on which the training of veterinary nurses is based.

The New Dogsteps: Understanding Gait, Rachel Page Elliot.

Obedience and Security Training for Dogs, Tom Scott (Popular Dogs).

Police Dogs: Training and Care (HMSO).

Practical Veterinary Nursing, G. Price (BSAVA).

Problem Dog: Behaviour and Misbehaviour, Dr Valerie O'Farell (Methuen).*

Running Puppy Classes, Erica Peachey.*

Running Your Own Boarding Kennels, Sheila Zabawa (Kogan Page).

The Story of Battersea Dogs Home, Gloria Cottesloe (David & Charles).

Think Dog, John Fisher (Witherby).*

Training the German Shepherd Dog, John Cree (Pelham).

Understanding Your Dog, Michael Fox. Out of print, but worth tracking down an old copy.

Understanding Your Dog, Peter Messant.

A Way of Life: Sheepdog Training, Handling and Trialling, Glyn Jones (Farming Press).

Your Dog: Its Behaviour, Development and Training, John Rogerson (Pelham).*

*Available from the APBC, 257 Royal College Street, London NW1.

VIDEOS

Dominant Dog, John Rogerson.

Training the Companion Dog, Dr Ian Dunbar.

Training the Dog in the Human Pack, John Fisher.

PERIODICALS

Weekly publications

Dog World, 9 Tufton Street, Ashford, Kent TN23 1QN.

Our Dogs, Our Dogs Publishing Co Ltd, 5 Oxford Road, Station Approach, Manchester M60 1SX.

Dog Training Weekly, 4/5 Feidr Castell Business Park, Fishguard, Pembrokeshire SA65 9BB.

Monthly or longer

Dogs Today, 6 Station Parade, Sunningdale, Berkshire SL5 0EP.

Kennel Gazette, 1-5 Clarges Street, Piccadilly, London W1Y 8AB.

Dogs Monthly, Ascot House, High Street, Ascot, Berkshire.

Pet Dogs Magazine, PO Box B163, Huddersfield, HD4 7YZ.

Kennel & Cattery Management, PO Box 193, Dorking, Surrey RH5 5YF.

Wild About Animals, Unit 3 Kingsgate Business Centre, Kingston, Surrey KT2 5AA.

Obedience Competitor, Long Meadows, Mooredges, Thorne, Doncaster, S. Yorks DN8 5RY.

Other Useful Addresses

In addition to those listed under individual entries:

Society of Companion Animal Studies (SCAS)
1a Hilton Road
Milngavie
Glasgow G62 7DN

Pet & Trade Industry Association
Bedford Business Centre
170 Mile Road
Bedford MK42 9TW
Tel: (01234) 273933

Universities Federation for Animal Welfare (UFAW)
8 Hamilton Close
South Mimms
Potters Bar
Hertfordshire EN6 3QD

People's Dispensary for Sick Animals (PDSA)
Whitechapel Way
Priorslee
Telford
Shropshire TF2 9PQ

Wood Green Animal Shelters
Kings Bush Farm
London Road
Huntingdon
Cambridgeshire PE18 8LJ

British Police & Services Canine Association
PO Box 2078
Edgbaston
Birmingham B16 8QZ
Tel: (0121) 455 9855

Bookworld Rugby
53 Bridget Street
Rugby
Warwickshire
Tel: (01788) 572643

WTM Publishing (books & videos on all aspects of dog training)
16 Hartlip Hill
Hartlip
Nr Sittingbourne
Kent ME9 7PA
Tel: (01795) 843892

Index